TROUT FISHING

TROUT FISHING

Trevor Housby

BLANDFORD PRESS
POOLE · DORSET

Series Editor: Jonathan Grimwood
Illustrations by: Anita Lawrence

First published in the U.K. 1985 by Blandford Press,
Link House, West Street, Poole, Dorset, BH15 1LL.

Copyright © 1985 Blandford Press Ltd

Distributed in the United States by
Sterling Publishing Co., Inc.,
2 Park Avenue, New York, N.Y. 10016.

British Library Cataloguing in Publication Data

Housby, Trevor
  Trout-fishing.
    1. Trout fishing   2. Fly fishing
    I. Title
    799.1′755   SH687

ISBN 0 7137 1607-X

Typeset by Megaron Typesetting, Bournemouth

Printed in Spain by Gryelmo, Bilbao

Contents

Dedicated
to my son Russell James Housby
may he always continue to fish

Introduction

During the past decade trout fisheries of the 'put and take' variety have sprung up in their hundreds. This has meant that the average angler in the street now has the opportunity to trout fish on a wide variety of still waters, most of which can be fished at reasonable cost. The emergence of such fisheries has naturally made a vast inroad into the traditions of trout fishing. New flies and lures have been devised, and tackle manufacturers have improved their rod, reel and line design to suit the new casting and fishing techniques which have become standard practice throughout the fly fishing world. My contribution to the scene was to develop the now universally used 'Dog Nobbler', a fly which has become a 'more than standard' pattern on most waters, from rivers to reservoirs, from small lakes to large pits.

In this book you will find a chapter devoted specifically to this particular fly. I hope this chapter will explain clearly the many uses of the Nobbler, although every angler and every angling writer who specialises in trout fishing has their own preferred way of using this fly. Basically, the truth is that the Dog Nobbler will catch fish at all times of the season, and in Britain the fishery reports that appear in *Angling Times, Trout fisherman* and *Anglers Mail* invariably quote this fly as the major fish catcher of each season.

This book will, I hope, both teach the novice angler and appeal to the experienced trout fisherman, for in it I have included many personal 'fish-landed-or-lost' stories, stories

Author with beautiful 14 pounder from River Test.

which are backed up by photographs. Trout fishing is now for everyone – popular across the world – and most anglers are now within easy travelling distance of a good fishery. Hopefully in future seasons many of us will meet on such waters.

Trevor Housby
Hampshire

Tackle – Getting Started

The basic equipment needed to start fly fishing is a rod, reel, fly line and a 'cast' or 'leader', plus a small selection of dry flies, wet flies and lures. Both the rod and the line will have been specially designed to help the angler make long accurate casts. Every fly rod made is designed for use with a particular recommended weight or 'rating' of fly line.

Some of the more modern rods can be used with a wide range of line weight ratings. But in my experience most of these perform best when used with the heaviest stipulated line.

For example, I own and use an 11 foot 4 inch carbon rod which the makers claim can be used with lines rated between no. 5 and no. 8 (lightish to fairly heavy). However, field tests show that the rod will cast a number 8 line perfectly but performs badly with lines rated 5, 6 and 7.

Rods

Fly rods vary greatly in price, what they are made from and performance. They are normally made in either two or three sections. In my opinion, a two section rod has a better casting action than a three section rod but, obviously, in the case of long fly rods a three section weapon is easier to store and carry.

Choosing a fly rod is seldom easy. Experienced anglers will know exactly which style of rod fits their own personal casting style. The novice, however, may well choose the wrong rod.

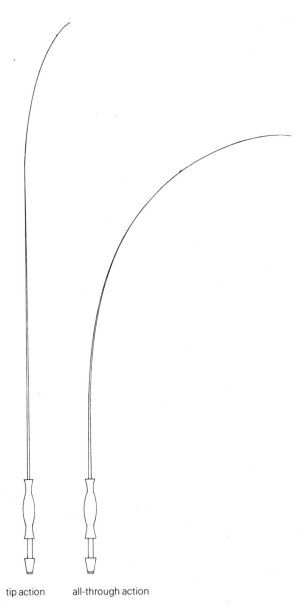

tip action   all-through action

FIGURE 1   Carbon fly rods. A tip-actioned rod is perfect for fast casting, while an all-through rod has a much slower action, reminiscent of cane. The number and weight of the rod rings alter the action of a rod blank: this is an important point to remember when purchasing a blank to make up your own rod.

For this reason my advice on rod selection is to choose and use a comparatively cheap rod for the first season and then – and only then – start to look for a more expensive weapon.

A hollow-glass rod of 8½ or 9 foot length, capable of casting a no. 7 or 8 line, makes the perfect starting rod. Once more experienced, an angler can select a rod to suit his (or her) own casting style.

'Tip-actioned' rods are ideal for the angler who has a fast or hurried casting style, while softer 'all-through action' rods (see Figure 1) are perfect for the angler who has a slow or relaxed casting style. This is because the time lapse between the back cast and forward cast is longer with a soft all-through rod than it is with a tip-actioned rod.

The action of a rod can be altered considerably by the number and weight of rod rings used. Too many heavy rings make a rod 'sloppy' in action: too few and the casting action can be badly impaired. Fly rods can be made from several materials, each material having its own particular characteristic. The main materials – in order of present importance – are as follows: carbon fibre, glass fibre, split cane and boron.

Carbon Fibre (Graphite)

Most fly fishermen now own and use a rod constructed from carbon fibre. All such rods are basically an admixture of carbon and fibre glass. Some rod makers claim a higher percentage of carbon content than others and thus a better action, but the majority of manufacturers give no details whatsoever about the carbon content of their rods.

When carbon was first introduced in the late 1970s the average price in Britain of such a rod was around £100. During the past two years, however, carbon content rods retailing at between £30 and £40 have flooded the market. Most of these are constructed from carbon blanks manufactured in the Far East and the majority represent extremely good value for money.

Carbon-fibre rods are lighter than similar rods constructed from glass fibre: a great advantage when you consider how long you are holding a rod during a day's fly fishing. Carbon rods are also slimmer in section than glass rods and much

A good bag from the carrier stream at Broadlands, taken on a glass fibre rod.

more powerful in their casting action. Anglers changing from glass to carbon fly rods often find that their casting distances increase substantially without additional effort being required.

Glass Fibre

For the beginner – or the angler who does not wish to incur too much initial expense – glass fibre is the ideal choice. Glass-fibre rods are light, strong, cheap and extremely forgiving in action. This makes them perfect for the inexperienced fly caster.

Split Cane

Although split cane is the traditional material used in fly-rod construction, few companies now manufacture such rods. A top quality split-cane fly rod from a company such as Hardys or Sharpes (both English made) commands a high price. In comparison to glass or carbon, split cane is difficult and time consuming to make, heavy to use, and has a soft casting action that does not suit most modern trout fishermen. Split cane rods also need constant maintenance to keep them in perfect condition and such care can be costly.

Boron

This was introduced in the early 1980s, supposedly as a replacement for carbon, but – so far – it has failed to make an impression on the market. It is slightly heavier than carbon and also more expensive.

Choosing A Rod

Choice of rod depends on the type of water to be fished. For example, tiny streams call for rods of between seven and eight feet in length; small stillwater fisheries for rods of between eight and nine and a half feet; and large reservoirs for rods of between nine and a half feet and eleven feet in length.

A 5 pound brownie taken on dry fly with a split cane rod.

Reels

There are dozens of fly reels on the market. These range from simple metal models to complex automatic reels or ultra-lightweight, ultra modern reels made of carbon or magnesium. Long discussions rage between anglers as to the exact matching of reel weight to rod weight, but most of this argument is unfounded.

The truth of the matter is that a fly reel is simply an accessory to the rod. It may be pleasing to look at or beautifully made; all the same, it serves little useful purpose except as a line store. As the actual playing of a fish is seldom done by winding in the reel, most experienced anglers prefer to 'strip' the line by hand.

Fly reels form three basic types: the single-action type where the drum moves one revolution for every turn of the handle; the multiplier type where the drum turns twice (or so, depending on the gearing) for every turn of the handle; and the clockwork or automatic type where the spool is driven by a spring. This last type winds itself up as you take line from the reel, slack line being recovered by pressing a button or lever which activates the spring mechanism and winds the line back in.

Choice of fly reel is up to each individual angler. One of the tried and trusted reels, the 'Rimfly' which is widely available is also one of the cheapest.

Few anglers actually use their reel for playing out a hooked trout, most preferring to play the fighting trout by taking in line or letting it out with the fingers of the left hand.

Novice anglers usually start by trying to wind their fish in, and often lose a good trout in the process. It takes practice and confidence to play a surging trout on line alone, but once achieved it is worth the effort. I have taken rainbow trout to 16 pounds 2 ounces without using the reel once during the fight. Even so, it is advisable to understand the various types of reels available and their usage.

Single-Action Reels

The average single-action reel is around three and a half inches in diameter. With the aim of getting the fastest possible recovery, the spool is sometimes so narrow that you cannot get your finger between the flanges to control the spool when the fish runs. This can be a problem and is something to watch out for and avoid.

To overcome this problem the spool edge is sometimes swept up and over the outer edge of the reel frame. This 'exposed-rim' spool makes a readily accessible braking surface but it is not without disadvantages. Most reels are made of aluminium, and a hard knock can easily damage the reel rim without it being noticeable to the angler.

If a hooked fish starts to take line, a dent in the rim can cause the reel to seize up, which in turn usually causes the leader to part instantly and loses you the fish.

Multiplier Reels

The multiplier is virtually identical in size and form to the single action, except that it is heavier and the handle is not fastened directly to the spool but is connected by a train of gears. These gears impart the multiplying action where one turn of the handle drives the spool round more than once.

To get the quickest possible recovery a high-gear ratio would seem to offer the best action but beware of reels that are over geared. The most usable gear ratio is less than 2:1.

Most single-action and multiplying fly reels have a permanent click-check to stop the spool over running. On better reels, the tension of this check is adjustable. The adjustment is made either by a milled screw, an adjustment cam or by moving the click spring across an adjusting rack. Each method works well.

Another feature found on better grade reels is the facility to change spools quickly, offering the opportunity for an angler to change quickly from one type of line to another.

Automatic reels

The automatic reel has no handle and line is recovered by a spring. The spring is wound up by the action of pulling line from the reel. When the angler wants to recover line he releases a trigger and the line is rapidly wound back (20 yards is rewound in approximately five seconds).

Automatic reels are, in my opinion, rather heavy and more

17

than a little gimmicky; although they are widely used in Europe and are very popular in the USA.

Any fly reel, whether it is single action, multiplier or an automatic should be fitted with a line guard. Without this, the action of stripping out line will quickly wear a groove in the reel frame which in turn will damage the line.

To function correctly a reel should hold a full length of fly line plus a minimum of 50 yards of backing line.

Fly Lines

Early fly lines were made of pure silk which was plaited, tapered and dressed with linseed oil. These oil-dressed silk lines were in universal use for three-quarters of a century: from the late nineteenth century to the middle of the twentieth. Then they were replaced by modern plastic-coated fly lines of plaited dacron overlayed with a coating of polyvinyl chloride (PVC).

For 'sinking' fly lines the PVC is impregnated with powdered metal, the quantity used determining the rate at which the line sinks. PVC is a hard material, and for this reason fly lines contain a suitable 'plasticiser' which is introduced during manufacture.

A wide range of lines are now available, all identified by a code known as the AFTM (American Federation of Tackle Manufacturers) system. The lines are listed from 1 to 12. The heavier the line the higher the rating number. The code tells you the kind of taper the line has (see Figure 2), the weight of the first 30 feet of the line and whether the line is a floating or a sinking one. Level lines are cheap to buy, unpleasant to use and have little to recommend them.

Line coding – AFTM

Abbreviations

L = level line
DT = double taper
WF = weight forward
ST = shooting head
F = floating
F/S = fast sinking, wet tip
VFS = very fast sinking

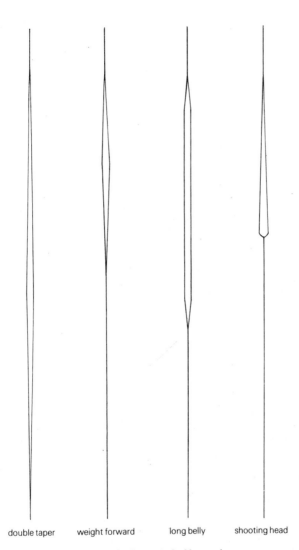

| double taper | weight forward | long belly | shooting head |

FIGURE 2   Different tapers for fly lines. A *double taper* is not as easy to cast as a weight forward but has a much gentler presentation and is ideal for river work or fishing shortish distances with light lines. A *weight forward* casts further than the previous line and is a popular line for small to medium stillwaters: handled carefully a reasonably delicate presentation can be achieved. The *long belly* was developed from the weight forward and its long mid-section allows more than the first thirty feet of line to be aerialised without using the thin running line normally found behind a forward taper, in theory this allows for better turnover. The *shooting head* is half a forward taper attached to a backing line of nylon monofilament and, as its name suggests, when used with the 'double-haul' technique, it allows an angler to shoot line for distances of 50 yards or more.

Examples
ST-8-S = shooting head, no. 8 line, sinking
DT-6-F = double taper no. 6 line, floating

Double Taper Lines

Double taper lines (designated DT) have both their ends tapered for more than 10 feet, giving a fine end to the line which falls more lightly on the water. Another advantage of a double taper is that when one end is worn the line can be reversed on your reel and you can then use the other end. The disadvantage is that they are not as easy to cast as weight forward lines.

Forward Taper Lines

Otherwise known as 'weight forward' (WF) lines, these resemble the first 30 feet or so of a double taper line with 40 feet of very fine fly line attached to the rear end. This allows more line to be 'shot' (passed) through the rings when casting. WF lines have recently been introduced with the first, heavier part being longer than the standard 30 feet. These are called 'long belly lines'.

The 'shooting head' is similar in principle to a 'forward taper line' and is a development from it, but instead of the fine shooting line at the rear end being a continuation of the PVC-coated fly line, it consists of nylon or dacron monofilament attached to the fly line by a special knot.

This allows even more line to be 'shot' in casting and, as the shooting head is usually cut from a double taper, they are much cheaper than either double or forward taper lines.

Most tackle shops sell half double tapers for making shooting heads, these will often need a further reduction in length, usually to 30-36 feet.

All of the above lines can be of various floating or sinking qualities. There are floaters, slow sinkers, medium sinkers and fast sinkers, as well as floating lines with sinking tips. They are all available in a range of weights, numbered 3 to 12. The more powerful your rod the heavier the line it will need.

Shooting Heads

As already mentioned the shooting head is simply a variation on the forward taper theme, whereby the actual fly line is restricted in length to that needed to give the rod its correct action – usually around 25-35 feet. This short section is spliced to a backing line, generally of nylon monofilament, which can have a circular or oval cross section. The oval cross section is far more resistant to tangling; which is the only real disadvantage of using monofilament as a backing material.

This set up of shooting head and monofilament backing line is ideally suited to long distance casting techniques such as the 'double haul', enabling experienced casters to cast 50 yards or more with ease.

Torpedo and Long Belly Lines

Just as the shooting head is merely a variation of the forward taper line, so there are other variations, such as the torpedo taper and the long belly, although the basic principle remains virtually the same in every case.

That section of the line which carries the weight necessary to action the rod correctly – and so enable efficient casting – is found towards one (forward) end of the line, so that the line is no longer reversible, unlike the double taper.

Line Densities

Manufacturers have developed their own specific descriptions for the line densities now produced and, in order not to confuse the issue for newcomers to fly fishing, it is probably as well to discuss individually the densities now in common use, offering brief comments on the function of each.

Floating Lines

For dry fly and nymph fishing, floating lines are essential. (Sinking lines are mainly for lake and reservoir fishing, when wet flies and lures of various kinds are needed.)

Floating lines are also perfect for the presentation of sunken flies which either require little working through the water or else require to be worked very close to the surface, either in a still water or on a slow flowing river.

The depth at which a sunken wet fly or nymph can be fished in a stillwater is restricted by the length of the cast (leader); on average some 9 to 12 feet.

It takes quite a while for an unweighted nymph to sink to that depth, and when trout are feeding close to the bed of a lake, it is common practice to use a nymph with a dressing containing lead or copper wire to speed the sink.

On the other hand, when trout are feeding above the bottom, application of floatant to part of the line end of the nylon leader will ensure that the fly does not sink too deep.

Occasionally, when the trout are feeding at the surface, a lure is fished on a floating line and stripped back so quickly that it skips across the surface, creating a definite wake. The Muddler Minnow is a perfect example of a wake fly, although many reservoir anglers use American Bugs for this style of surface fishing.

Neutral Density Lines

Sometimes called Intermediate lines, these sink very slowly at about 1 foot every 12 seconds. They are ideal for fishing nymphs just under the surface and are good in a crosswind as they do not drag on the surface.

Sink Tip Lines

These lines are carefully manufactured so that the 10 foot tip – which sinks at medium rate – is supported by the longer floating body of the line.

When fishing a nymph in deepish water with a sink tip, the 'take' is signalled by slight movement of the floating section. The line is equally efficient at indicating a take as the fly sinks.

This type of line can also be very effective in deeper or medium-flowing rivers, where it is vital that depth is achieved quickly and maintained, or in stillwaters where the margins are full of snags which would foul a full sinking line.

Some anglers find difficulty in casting a sink tip line because of the imbalance between the dense tip and the less dense body, but this can usually be overcome by practise.

Two beautiful trout for Bill Sibbons, taken on a dry line.

Slow Sinking Lines

The use of a slow sinker does not differ greatly in technique from use of a sink tip, for it can be used to take fish on the drop, or at a slow-to-medium speed retrieve, in stillwaters and in deeper rivers. Nymphs can be fished on slow sinkers, but lures are more commonly used with this line. The take of a fish is signalled – as with all sinking lines – by a hard pull, transmitted to the retrieving hand. These lines sink at a rate of about 1 foot every 8 seconds.

Medium Sinking Lines

Medium sinkers obviously sink faster than slow sinkers, and are better suited to fishing in deeper or faster water. However with maximum-speed lure stripping – bringing the lure in very fast – the lure itself will rise very close to the surface, which can be an advantage when trout are working in the upper levels of the water but demand a fast moving lure which does not break the surface. Medium sinking lines sink at a rate of about 1 foot every 6 seconds.

Fast Sinking Lines

Fast sinkers enable fast working of a fly in deep water and ensure that, no matter how fast the retrieve, the lure will be unlikely to rise above midwater. These lines are best suited to fast-flowing rivers or to deep stillwaters where the fish are inclined to feed close to the bottom. These lines sink at a rate of about 1 foot every 3 seconds.

Very Fast Sinking Lines

Very fast sinking lines often carry lead in the core. They are ideal for the deep reservoirs, lakes and lochs where the fish feed deep, and where it is important that a lure stripped quickly does not rise much above the bottom. They are ideal for use in fast-flowing rivers, for they enable the angler to remain in close touch with his fly throughout each cast. They sink at a rate of about 1 foot a second.

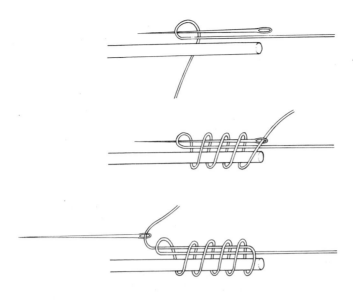

needle knot

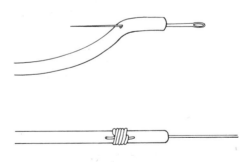

modified needle knot

FIGURE 3   A needle knot is ideal for attaching backing to a fly line or fly line to a leader. To tie this knot a darning needle is held (in the left hand, if right handed) parallel to the fly line and a leader bent back on itself and wound four times round the fly line, the fourth turn being passed through the eye of the needle, and the needle pulled through.

For a tidier knot, pass the needle up through the centre of the fly line (or backing, if fitting fly line to hollow braided backing) and out through the side, thread the leader through the resultant hole and tie the knot as for above. This gives a tidier, and stronger, end result.

25

The level lead-cored line is without doubt the fastest sinker of all at over a foot a second. This is not used for conventional fly casting but for trolling behind a moving boat. The technique used is to drag the largest size of lure available at a regular speed across the bottom where, hopefully, it will attract very large trout which have adopted a bottom feeding existence.

Although hardly fly fishing as such, this technique is popular with boat-fishing reservoir anglers.

Backing Lines

For most kinds of fly fishing a fly will will need backing of some sort. Monofilament or braided dacron line is wound on to the reel first, and then the coated fly line is attached to the backing. Flattened monofilament with a breaking strain of about 25 pounds, or special monofilament sold for backing purposes, is cheaper than braided backing line and easier to connect securely to the fly line.

Monofilament backing line is attached to the fly line with a needle knot (see Figure 3). The same knot – with a slight variation – can be used to tie a short piece of ordinary round-section monofilament to the other (forward) end of the fly line to which, in turn, the tapered leader (cast) can be knotted with another needle knot, a three turn blood knot or a double grinner knot (see Figure 4). All these knots pass easily through the rod rings.

Leaders (Casts)

Obviously a fly is never attached directly to the fly line. Instead a thinner line – called the leader – joins the fly to the reel line.

The leader is where the action is and the point, the last few feet at the end of the leader, is where the action starts. Too thick a point and fish shy off or take short: too fine a point and the action is dead in seconds, when leader and point part company!

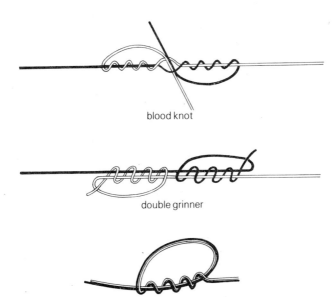

blood knot

double grinner

four turn water knot

FIGURE 4   Other essential knots for fly fishing. The *blood knot* can be used to attach two parts of a leader, or to make droppers. The *water knot* is ideal for attaching lengths of nylon of varying thickness to each other, and can also be used for droppers. The *double grinner* is probably the strongest knot there is for attaching nylon to nylon and is useful for tying a leader to a leader snood (the short bit of nylon monofilament already fastened by a needle knot to the flyline, to which the leader is then fastened).

With a fish on the leader, the point must be able to withstand every underwater surge of its muscle-packed body, every slash of a leaping trout jerking its head to throw the hook. The leader must survive the twisting and wrenching of the hook in its nylon knot socket, it must stretch and recoil to absorb shocks before they hit the rod tip and certainly before the angler reacts.

All this is expected of a piece of nylon some 0.15 mm in diameter for a point with a 3 pound breaking strain. At 4 pounds breaking strain, the point is still only 0.18 mm and even at 7 pounds the point has a diameter of only 0.225 mm.

For dry fly fishing, where perfect presentation is required, a tapering leader should be used. These tapered leaders can be made up at home by using four or more equal lengths of nylon of diminishing poundage knotted together. When I make up a tapered leader of this kind I use nylon of 9, 7, 5 and 3 pounds breaking strain. Each section being joined by a standard blood knot.

Knotless tapered leaders can be obtained from all fishing tackle shops but they do tend to be expensive. The commercially-produced knotless leader is at its most useful for dry fly work on rivers, where fish tend to be line shy, as the knotless cast helps to roll the fly out neatly beyond the fly line. This keeps the line behind the fish where with luck it will remain unnoticed.

For wet fly fishing a taperless leader with three or even four dropper knots can be used (see Figure 5) which will allow the angler to use a team of flies. This technique is particularly effective when boat fishing in lakes, lochs or reservoirs.

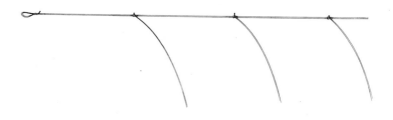

FIGURE 5   A three-droppered taperless leader is perfect for wet fly fishing and the droppers can be attached with a blood knot or a water knot.
    Fishing with droppers allows a fisherman to set the flies at various depths and so find the level at which trout are feeding. Problems start when more than one dropper fly is taken at the same time!

Tapered leaders are not essential for lure fishing. Most experienced anglers prefer to use a level line taken directly from a spool of nylon. For all round use, a line of 5 pound breaking strain makes perfect leader material but when fishing in lakes or reservoirs noted for big trout then use nylon with a breaking strain of 7 or even 9 pounds.

A hundred yards/metres of good quality nylon currently costs about £1. At that rate a point costs about a penny. What is the purpose of a £100 or more worth of carbon-fibre rod and magnesium reel if a pennyworth of nylon fails? There is absolutely no sense in using last year's nylon or leftover leaders.

Above all, it is vitally important to change a point or leader whenever there is reason to doubt it. If it kinks, twists, necks or gathers a wind knot (a knot which appears in a leader as if by magic), take no chances – get rid of it.

Most leaders are between 9 and 15 foot long from butt to point. A knotted, tapered leader is usually composed of three, four or five pieces of nylon, each with a progressively smaller diameter, joined together with knots. One or several droppers (flies set above the 'terminal' or 'point fly') may be attached to this by more knots.

With so many knots to be tied and relied upon, you must be quite confident of your knotmanship. Alternatively, you could rely on someone else's skill and buy made up leaders, but most competent trout fishermen prefer to tie their own.

Use knots in which you have faith. The ordinary dropper knot will not let you down, but it is tricky to tie, especially at the waterside. If you have trouble with it use the water knot which is easy to make. Many people tie this knot with as many as a dozen turns, but four are adequate.

An expensive alternative to all this is to use manufactured knotless tapers either for the whole leader or – and this is cheaper – just for the tail end and tie on the point yourself. These tapers turn over sweetly, reduce the risk of tangles during casting in gusty weather and are available in a variety of sizes. In fact they are excellent – but you cannot buy them for a penny a yard!

Hooks

Hooks come in a wide variety of shapes and sizes (see Figure 6). Dry flies are traditionally tied on up-eyed hooks. This sort of hook allows the very tip of the leader to rest lightly on the surface of the water where it will not sink and cause the

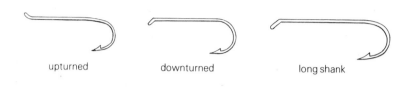

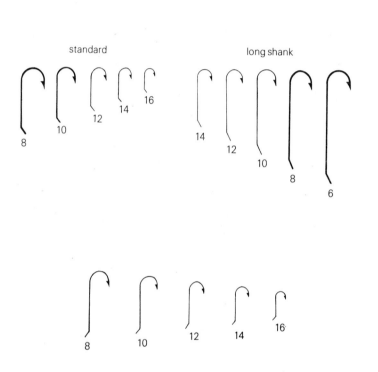

FIGURE 6 Hook varieties and sizes. Dry flies are traditionally tied on upturned hooks, to allow a leader to sit on the surface rather than drag and pull the fly down. Wet flies are normally tied on downturned standard (normal shank) hooks, while most nymphs and lures are tied on downturned, longshank hooks.

For trout fishing, sizes 16 standard to 8 longshank should be sufficient; and indeed many waters now place their upper limit at 8 longshank.

floating fly to skate, or drag the fly across or under the surface.

Wet flies, nymphs and lures are tied on down-eyed hooks. All these are designed to fish under the surface where perfect presentation is not a critical factor.

Hooks are coded by size. The larger the number the smaller the hook. Dry flies and nymphs can be tied on hooks down to size 22, while lures tend to be tied on size 8 or 10 hooks. (Size 8 is often the upper limit on a water.) To make matters more complex, most hooks can be obtained in long, medium (standard) and short shanked versions. A longshank, size 10 hook is approximately twice the size of a shortshank size 10. Sooner or later most fly fishermen turn their hand to fly tying, and it is at this stage that hook sizes, shapes and codes really become of interest.

The Trout Fly Revolution

During the last twenty years there has been a revolution in fly fishing. Apart from the dramatic changes in equipment – twenty years ago split cane was still king – involving carbon rods, shooting heads, lightweight reels, etc, the greatest change of all has occurred in the flies themselves and the way we fish them.

This revolution has been brought about by the way fly fishing changed in emphasis from rivers and lochs to reservoirs and tailor-made stillwaters.

This greatly increased the numbers of trout fishermen, who then basically only had the modern reservoir lakes available to them. Which, in turn, meant having to learn to cast greater distances with the rod than the previous generations would have thought possible or necessary, and retrieve with the lure at far quicker rates than they would have imagined worthwhile.

There are, of course, still certain times when it is well worth reverting to a more traditional form of fly fishing – for example when sedge or midge hatches are occurring – and being able to cast to a rising fish will always be very satisfying, particularly so with the dry fly.

During the past two decades there have been numerous books on the developments in this sport. Several have been milestones like *Still Water Trout Fishing* by Tom Ivens, or Veniard's *Reservoir And Lake Flies* with its invaluable contributions from Richard Walker, Dave Collyer, etc, or

Opening day at Leominstead.

indeed Richard Walker's own book *Modern Trout Fishing*. All include fly dressings which cannot be improved upon, and still catch as many fish today as they did then.

I still tie the Walker's edge patterns and I have never found anything better. The same goes for his Mayfly Nymph and his Dun. Although the dressings have been changed over the years I still use the earlier dressing, with ostrich herl bodies and pheasant tails, using the pheasant tail to make the two brown rings in the lower abdomen. I have also had some success making up the Dun with a detached body.

Another very effective fly at times is Tom Ivens' Jersey Herd. A lure designed to be stripped back just under the surface without breaking through it. I tie the body of this fly with a gold coloured glitter wool. This must be easier than cutting a spiral strip from a 'Jersey' milk top which, in any case, is not practical when tying in large numbers.

The glitter wool idea came from an article by Taff Price in *Trout and Salmon* many years ago, and is an example of how an original and already good dressing can be changed without detriment to the fly.

This then is the basic Jersey Herd. Substitute wool for the dressings, leave out the hackle and you produce a Baby Doll, (white wool, small red wool thorax), plus a variety of patterns using different coloured wools.

Dry Flies

Dry fly fishing has always been regarded as the supreme art in fly fishing circles. This is particularly so on chalk streams, where accurate presentation of the fly is essential. Dry flies also play their part in reservoir and lake fishing, where trout also feed on surface insects.

Trout will rise to a variety of natural flies but, as far as the dry fly fisherman is concerned, the mayfly hatch has to be the favoured time. When the mayflies hatch they emerge from the water in such large numbers that trout become totally preoccupied with gorging themselves to capacity. Even the largest trout rise freely and on these occasions almost any artificial pattern representing a mayfly will take fish.

Early in the season, when hawthorn flies hatch in large numbers, good catches can be made with the aid of a Black

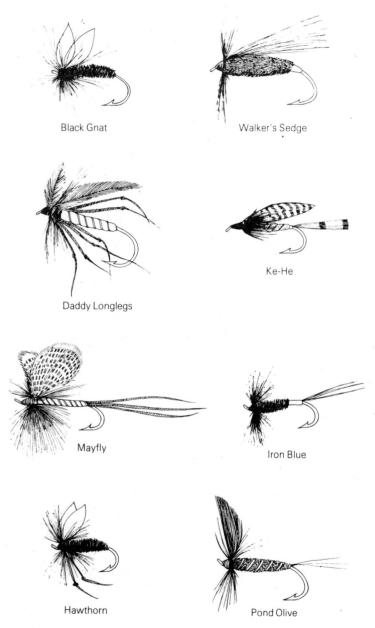

Black Gnat

Walker's Sedge

Daddy Longlegs

Ke-He

Mayfly

Iron Blue

Hawthorn

Pond Olive

FIGURE 7   Essential Dry Flies. (See pages 135-136 for patterns.)

Gnat or similar dark dry fly. Once again, this applies mostly to running waters but many lakes also have a good hatch of hawthorn fly. Kingsbridge Lakes near Poole in Dorset are a typical example of a British stillwater fishery that produces an excellent hawthorn fly hatch.

In late summer, one of the most popular flies to hatch on nearly every water is the sedge. These normally hatch in July and August, and they are present in ones and twos throughout the day and in vast numbers at nightfall. If weather conditions are good, and flies are hatching, a dry pattern representing a sedge can be very effective.

There are also hatches of buzzers (midges) throughout the year and a number of ephemerids, such as the olives, etc, also hatch.

Many land-borne insects are included in the trout's diet sheet. These live and often breed on dry land but get blown onto the water by prevailing winds. These flies are particularly important to the reservoir and loch angler, because a large expanse of water is often too great for these insects to fly across in safety and so they get trapped in the surface. Of the insects that hatch on the land, the daddy longlegs (crane fly) is the one which adds most substantially to the larder of the trout. In late summer, 'daddies' hatch in vast numbers in bankside vegetation and, being weak fliers, are readily carried onto the water when the wind rises. The trout know this and cruise the margins or wind lanes sucking in daddy longlegs (crane flies) as they fall.

Up in Orkney, the Ke-He fly – tied to represent a tiny bee – is a great killer but each area of every country has its special land-borne flies – known locally – which can produce excellent results.

Another land insect that really interests trout is the flying ant. Swarms of these insects are occasionally blown onto the water and when this happens the trout feed heavily on them: so it is wise to have a suitable imitation in your fly box.

In almost all instances where trout feed on land-borne insects the rule is not to move the fly. An imitation is far more likely to succeed if it is cast out and then left.

Regarding patterns of fly that are essential to dry fly fishing, every angler should include the following: Tup's Indispensible; Mayfly; Sedge; Black Gnat; Ke-He; Iron Blue;

Mallard and Claret

Teal and Silver

Silver March Brown

Invicta

Wickham's Fancy

Black Zulu

Black and Peacock Spider

Black Pennell

FIGURE 8   Essential Wet Flies. (See pages 136-139 for patterns.)

Daddy Longlegs; Sherry Spinner; Pond (or Lake) Olive; Lunn's Particular; and Flying Ant. Equipped with these in varying sizes an angler should be able to deal with almost every circumstance likely to be met on any type of trout water.

Wet Flies

In contrast to the dry fly, which simulates an insect floating on the water's surface, the wet fly is used to imitate a small insect or creature living and moving below the surface.

This difference of function is reflected in the manner of tying the fly and in the materials used, for although some fly patterns can be tied for either dry or wet fly fishing, each has its own distinctive features.

Stiff cock hackles are necessary for a floating fly, but softer water-absorbent hackles help the wet fly to sink as well as providing movement when the fly is working, by the action of the stream or during the retrieve.

Wet flies can be wingless, fully hackled or with 'spider-type' hackles, or even with reduced and lighter hackles according to type.

Winged Wet Flies

The winged wet flies are the best known patterns. Flies such as the Mallard and Claret and the Teal and Silver can be tied in variations of colour, providing useful alternatives: Mallard and Claret, Mallard and Black, Mallard and Mixed, etc. Other equally popular and effective winged flies are the Golden Olive and the Silver March Brown. These are normally tied with reduced throat hackles.

Palmered Flies

Some winged flies are tied with full hackles wound along the entire length of the hook shank, and even with small additional 'throat' hackles as well. Invicta and Wickham's Fancy are typical examples.

Flies tied with the hackle extending along the length of the

Walker's Mayfly Nymph

Damselfly Nymph

Pheasant Tail Nymph

Corixa

FIGURE 9   Essential Nymphs (See pages 138-139 for patterns.)

body are said to be palmered, after the 'palmer', which may be black. An excellent example of this type is the Zulu.

Spider Hackled Flies

A further group of important wingless flies is typified by the Black and Peacock Spider, an excellent fly when fish are feeding on snail. The Snipe and Purple, and the Partridge and Orange are also of this type.

Nymphs

Nymphs are very different to dry or wet flies in make up, appearance and function. They are intended to represent the larval (nymph) form of many differing underwater insects. The best known are probably Walker's Mayfly Nymph, the Damselfly Nymph and the Pheasant Tail Nymph. All are extremely effective patterns and take their share of fish. There are also green nymphs, brown nymphs and black nymphs, all excellent if used in the right place at the right time.

Nymphs are usually tied with an imitation thorax and wing case, as well as having a banded or ringed appearance, to represent the segmented abdomen common in many natural nymph forms. They may also have tiny hackles or hairs built in to the thorax to give a visual suggestion of moving limbs.

Other nymphs are used to represent small water beetles that are common in many waters. The Corixa, tied with imitation hard wing cases, is a popular and successful example of this pattern.

Within each of the groups described above there are a few examples intended to be accurate imitations of the natural insect. But the others are intended to suggest a whole group of similar, insect-like and edible-looking creatures.

Lures

These are basically attractor patterns, tied on long-shanked hooks (identical to nymph hooks) or on two or three small hooks tied in twos. They are now the most widely used of all fly patterns available and account for more trout than wet flies or nymphs.

Lures can be anything in length from one to three inches, with flashy or coloured bodies and large wings over the shank: typical and successful examples are the Ace of Spades, the Appetizer and the Muddler Minnow.

Other important artificials are the distinctive group made up with gold or silver tinsel, or with brilliant fluorescent colours: the Jersey Herd is of this kind.

Wet Fly/Lure Action

The success of the wet fly or lure often depends far more on its action in the water than on its resemblance or otherwise to a particular insect. When trout are on the feed the actual pattern is not important, but when the fish are preoccupied or need tempting the angler must use ingenuity to discover what the

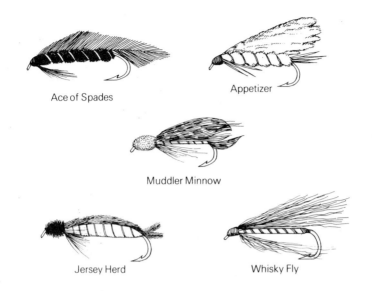

Ace of Spades

Appetizer

Muddler Minnow

Jersey Herd

Whisky Fly

FIGURE 10   Essential Lures. (See pages 139-141 for patterns.)

fish are feeding on, and which colour they are taking.

Unlike his dry fly counterpart, the wet fly angler may fish two or three flies on the same cast, the extra flies being attached to droppers off the cast at intervals of 4 or 5 feet. The patterns are selected so that the tail fly (point fly) can be fished deep, with the bottom dropper in midwater, and the top dropper near to the surface.

An angler can even arrange for the top dropper (fly on a short cast) to dibble above the surface while fishing the other flies below it. This is particularly true of loch fishing, where 'teams' of flies are still commonly employed.

Modern still water 'put-and-take' fisheries usually have a one fly rule. Rightly so, for when 'stockies' (stocked fish) go on the feed each fly can be taken. A situation which rarely occurs when wild loch fish are the quarry.

A Fly For All Seasons –
The Dog Nobbler

Like it or not, modern trout fishing is a competitive sport. Most anglers fish day ticket waters: put and take fisheries that operate on regular (sometimes daily or weekly) stockings, with fish weighing from 1½ pounds upwards being introduced throughout the season.

When first released stock fish can be easy to catch. Give them a few days to acclimatise, however, and they quickly become wary. This is particularly true on heavily fished waters where the fish are often hooked and lost or simply frightened by intensive angling activity.

Once trout have learned about danger they become extremely difficult to catch. And naturally it is the largest fish that learn these lessons the hard way. A big fish is usually a visible fish. Visibility means that in its first few hours or days of freedom it is often stalked by dozens of anglers and bombarded by hundreds of flies, lures or nymphs. If the newly-introduced big fish survives this intensive bombardment it becomes very difficult to tempt with artificial flies.

Every trout water in Britain holds such fish, often in large numbers, and I am the sort of angler who invariably wants to catch large fish. On many occasions this has led to me being dubbed a 'meat hunter': roughly translated this means a trout fisherman who wants to catch the maximum weight of good fish possible on each fishery.

The sort of anglers who call me these names and look down on my fishing activities are the sort of anglers who seldom catch fish. My interest is in results. I certainly do not believe in killing for the sake of killing or size for the sake of size, but I do

Author with his Nobbler-covered hat and a 12 pound 13 ounce rainbow from Nythe Lake.

believe in being an efficient angler, with big fish being a challenge and my main target.

Selective fishing of this kind is seldom easy, particularly when the fish concerned have already learned to fear both the angler and his fly. For a number of seasons I concentrated hard on catching these large trout, and this ultimately led me to the development of the 'Dog Nobbler' lure. A lure which has now become a standard pattern among lake and reservoir anglers, particularly where big fish are concerned.

Dog Nobbler

FIGURE 11   *The* Essential Lure. The Dog Nobbler, tied in a variety of colours, takes large trout throughout the season on both sinking and floating lines. Used with a sinking line and a short, fast 'chopping' retrieve it proves deadly for 'double figure' fish.

The list of successes chalked up to the Dog Nobbler is far too long to outline at length, but I have taken rainbow trout to 16 pounds 2 ounces on it; hundreds of limit bags; and upwards of twenty more double figure fish.

Many other anglers have done equally well. The Dog Nobbler won the 1982 French championship, and has accounted in Britain for many of the trout entered for the famed 'Trout Masters Contest' organised by *Trout fisherman* magazine. The 'Nobbler' has also been the subject of one *Out of Town* television film and has featured in many other television productions. While popular singer Frankie Vaughan – whom I have never met – is a keen trout angler and a total fan of the nobbler.

What then is so special about this lure? To answer this, first let me explain about the evolution of the Dog Nobbler.

Having become aware that most waters held large, apparently uncatchable trout I started to put my mind to the problems involved. I already knew that the majority of large trout spend most of their time in the deepest water, usually feeding within inches of the bottom. A visibly rising trout is usually a small trout: as big fish rarely (in my experience) surface feed.

For this reason, my inclination is to use a fast sinking line for much of my trout fishing. By using a line that sinks rapidly I get my fly down to fish level quickly, which means that in an average day's trout fishing I can cover much more ground than an angler using a line that sinks slowly.

Having established – to my own satisfaction – that big trout are basically bottom feeders I began to experiment with flies and lures. Two consistently successful patterns soon emerged: the Muddler Minnow and the Whisky Fly. Neither have a natural movement in the water and to try to improve matters I added a tiny split shot directly in front of the fly. This was particularly effective when used in conjunction with the Muddler Minnow. The buoyant deer-haired head of the muddler, counter-balanced by the single split shot, gave the lure a seductive dipping motion on the retrieve. A movement which produced far more fish of higher average size than normal.

Soon after this discovery, I was fishing in America and discovered that bass anglers use a lead headed lure, called a

A 16 pound 2 ounce rainbow taken on a Dog Nobbler, the author's best weight to date.

Author with a bright rainbow.

jig, which works on a similar principle. On my return to
England I began to tie lures on the jig principle, with the split
shot actually crimped and glued to the shank of the hook.

My first patterns were tied very roughly, using chenille for
the thorax of the fly, and ostrich herl for the tail. To assess the
effectiveness of these lures I tried them out on a deep clear-
water stream where I could watch the reaction of the trout. To
say I learned a lot would be an understatement. Even the early
prototypes of the Dog Nobbler were lethal.

I quickly realised that trout regarded the fly as a mixture of
food and a threat to their territorial rights. If the trout were
hungry they simply ate the fly. If they did not want to eat, they
would invariably sweep out aggressively to threaten the lure.
If the lure then reappeared they would invariably take it
savagely, and even fish which came off the hook would turn
and attack the lure for a second time.

During these visual experiments I learned a great deal about
both fish and fly. I realised from the outset that the lure – if
properly developed – would ultimately become a winner. So

I set about improving and modifying the pattern until I was satisfied that it would catch a fish under all circumstances.

What I was looking for was a 'superfly' that attracted and took fish first by action, second by colour. I knew that if I could achieve the perfect movement, I only needed a range of colour variants and I would have a fly for all seasons. This idea was in total opposition to all previous thoughts on fly fishing.

Traditionally the trout angler has tied and used a fly to resemble a natural insect or water creature. 'Matching the hatch' is a standard fly fishing term, and one that I had once strictly adhered to. Modern lure fishing had already gone some way towards dispelling much of the traditional lore surrounding trout flies but, even so, most lures were designed to imitate some creature found naturally in and around trout waters. Many lures were designed to look like the fry of perch, roach, stickleback, etc. These were highly effective when the trout became preoccupied with fry feeding, but usually only remained effective for short periods of time. The Dog Nobbler, however, was basically designed to aggravate the trout.

By nature all trout are aggressive and territorial and a lure which triggers this aggression is a lure that also activates the fish's instinct to attack and bite at an object that aggravates. In my opinion biting and feeding are the same thing. In either case, the trout takes the fly or lure into its mouth where with luck, the hook will take a firm hold.

I realised virtually from the onset, that the ostrich herl tail of the Nobbler was just not soft enough to achieve the full flowing movement which triggers off trout aggression.

Fortunately, finding the perfect tail material was simple. Marabou is readily available as a fly dressing material. A few strands of marabou made the perfect tail and the secret of the Dog Nobbler's success is in its long flowing tail.

When dry, a Nobbler looks like a fluffy miniature shaving brush. Immerse it in water and the tail immediately elongates, to give the fly an eel-like tail. Again, this goes contrary to all fly fishing theories. In the past most trout fishermen have always believed that a fly with a long tail is useless. The theory being that trout will 'take' the long tail section, and miss the hook completely. 'Taking short' has, in fact, become a standard saying among fly casters.

47

The Dog Nobbler totally destroys this theory, although initially many experienced anglers refused to try Nobbler patterns as they were convinced that the Nobbler would be unable to hook fish. The interesting thing about the Nobbler, however, is that trout are often hooked in the back of the throat or well inside the mouth. Proof that the undulating tail excites them into taking and attempting to swallow the fly completely.

One idea that I did get from the American bass jigs was to bend the shank of the hook down before attaching the shot (see Figure 12). This cranked hook shank has a number of advantages. The most important being as follows: one, in use the lure works upside down which makes it less likely to catch in weed or bottom debris; two, when a fish does take the fly, the hook is much more likely to engage than a conventional straight shanked hook.

standard longshank   'cranked' longshank

FIGURE 12   Making a Dog Nobbler (see page 58). Bend the shank of the hook to an angle of about 40° before attaching the lead shot or winding on lead wire for the head. This 'cranked' effect gives the Nobbler increased hooking power.

The fact that the hook shank is angled, means it acts like a plough shank to drive the hook point and barb deep into the trout, this is an important factor. Far too often an apparently well hooked fish will 'fall off' in the last stages of battle. With the increased hooking power of the cranked nobbler hook, such losses are rare.

As already said, the secret of the Nobbler's success lies in the movement of its flowing marabou tail. Even on a straight retrieve this 'tail action' can be readily seen and in the water the fly has all the movement of a small fish. Part of the fly's attraction also lies in the vibration ripples created by the forward motion of the fly. My feeling is that it is a mixture both of visual movement and sensed vibration that drives the trout wild.

Many anglers asked me why the fly is called a 'Dog Nobbler'? After all most flies have pretty, traditional names: Invicta, Teal and Blue, Peter Ross, Blue Charm, and so on. The name 'Nobbler' stems from two things. One, I have always called large wary trout 'Dogs' and two, my flies Nobble fish that in many cases would otherwise avoid capture: end product the name Dog Nobbler!

Originally I tied my own Nobblers but three seasons ago I authorised my old friend Syd Knight – the well known professional fly tier – to market this pattern of fly. The demand has been such that Syd ties over 30,000 of these to order each season. Various 'pirate' versions have also appeared on the market, but the only true pattern is that produced in England by Syd Knight of Bridgnorth.

Despite massive press and 'word of mouth' coverage there are many anglers who have still to try this fly. Success stories, however, are rife. A perfect example being one recounted by top fly caster Roy Buckland.

Several seasons ago Roy decided on a half day's fishing in Hampshire at Rooksbury Mill Trout Fishery near Andover. On arrival he found a number of other anglers in action, but none catching fish. Roy decided on this occasion to fish a yellow Nobbler and within two hours had caught his limit of five fish and was preparing to leave. Seeing his success two anglers approached him and asked about the fly. Both had heard of the Dog Nobbler but neither had even seen one.

Roy promptly handed over his fly and left the fishery. Two days later he was back and, on looking in the returns book, saw that both anglers had achieved limit bags of rainbow trout to 7 ½ pounds in weight. The fly had then been handed on to yet another frustrated angler who 'limited out' just as quickly. In one afternoon that yellow Dog Nobbler had taken four 5-fish limits. A total of twenty trout, weighing over 70 pounds in all. A typical example of this pattern taking big fish on a day when all else failed to catch.

Recently I had a similar experience while fishing Nythe Lake at Arlesford, also in Hampshire. During the morning I fished a Nobbler to selected fish seen cruising and had taken three fish to 6 pounds weight, when a party of anglers from

A fine brace for the author from Nythe Lake.

Sussex asked what fly I was using. When I told them the Dog Nobbler, they confessed that they had never heard of the fly. Naturally I gave them one – in this instance tied in brown – and then left the fishery for lunch.

On arrival back I found that the angler using the Nobbler had caught three nice fish and had then hooked a huge rainbow which promptly broke his leader. Yet again the Dog Nobbler had proved its capabilities, and won itself a new bag of converts.

Such stories are common and the Nobbler – even in its most basic form – has proved its ability to catch fish at any time in all conditions: truly a fly for all seasons.

Understanding The Dog Nobbler

To get the best out of any fly it is advisable to understand both the fly and its uses. The Nobbler will catch fish for any angler. In the hands of an expert, however, it is lethal.

I have used the Nobbler on floating and sinking lines, but believe that it catches best when used on the sinking line. Having cast out, the fly should then be allowed to sink down to the bottom. A short fast retrieve should be employed to get the best action from this fly. The faster the retrieve the better, using a short chopping stroke of the retrieving hand. At all times the forefinger of the rod hand should serve as a brake to the incoming line. When a take is felt, the line should be trapped briefly against the rod handle as the rod is lifted to set the hook. The forefinger can then be used as a sort of clutch, applying pressure when the fish shows signs of tiring, easing the pressure when the fish shows an inclination to run out line.

Dog Nobbler lures will catch fish no matter what method is used to retrieve the lure. The short chopping stroke described does, however, catch fish more consistently than any other method yet devised. No matter what fly is used, there are days when trout hit one colour in preference to another, and the Dog Nobbler is no exception to this rule. Some colours work best at certain seasons. The following details should help the angler to make a right choice.

1. Yellow Dog Nobbler

In my experience this is the best all round colour and the first choice. Yellow will work throughout the season, particularly on overcast days or when the water is coloured after rain.

2. White Dog Nobbler

Like the yellow pattern, the white nobbler is a consistent fish catcher. I like to use the white variant on bright days or – contrary to the traditional deep equals dark rule – in clear or extra deep water.

3. Orange Dog Nobbler

A good mid season or late season colour. It is particularly effective when algae growths turn the water a pea-soup colour.

4. Green Dog Nobbler

This colour will often produce fish when all else has failed. I seldom use it regularly – or as an early choice – but I have had some very fine fish on it.

5. Olive Dog Nobbler

This pattern with its olive green colour is particularly effective during mid to late summer, especially when damsel flies begin to hatch and the trout become preoccupied with damsel nymphs.

6. Brown Dog Nobbler

Brown is not my favourite colour but on occasion a brown Dog Nobbler can work wonders. I look on this pattern as a mid season standby. It works best on waters containing leeches.

7. Black Dog Nobbler

Black is always a good fish-catching colour. It is most effective for large brown trout, although on occasion rainbow trout will also take black in preference to all other colours.

8. Tiger Dog Nobblers

The so-called Tiger Nobblers are tied in exactly the same way as standard Nobbler patterns. The difference is that instead of being one colour only, they are tied in mixed colours. A typical example has a chocolate brown body with a yellow and white tail. However, any colour combination can be used.

9. Mayfly Nymph Nobbler

Introduced in 1981, this Nobbler version of Richard Walker's Mayfly Nymph proved an instant success when the combination of traditional Mayfly Nymph colour and rippling Nobbler tail proved lethal.

10. Palmered Dog Nobbler

These are simply palmered versions (see Figure 13) of the standard Dog Nobbler patterns. The palmered body hackles give the effect of 'breathing' as the fly is retrieved. This additional movement can be extremely effective, particularly on hard fished waters.

Palmered Nobbler

FIGURE 13   A Palmered Nobbler. This variation does well at times, as the body hackle gives the fly an impression of 'breathing'. Tie a feather in at the tail of the Nobbler and wind it up the body then fasten down with wire tinsel.

Casting The Dog Nobbler

All Dog Nobblers are leaded. Some patterns having lead wire built into the head section, others have heads made of lead shot (see Figure 11). The former patterns are easy enough to cast but the lead shot versions are not. The trick to casting a shotted Nobbler is to cut down on leader length. With a heavy Nobbler I rarely use a leader of more than eight feet in length and often use leaders of no more than six feet. The short leader then stops the fly from dropping too fast during the forward cast and avoids making a splash.

Using The Nobbler At Close Range

On many trout fisheries it is possible to stalk and catch trout at close range. Trout are usually territorial fish. This is particularly true of the larger specimens which often take up residence close in to a bank.

A trout which has established a territory may be difficult to catch on conventional fly patterns and techniques. Under these circumstances a Dog Nobbler can be highly effective. The trick is to flip the lure out on leader length alone: only a yard or two of actual fly line should project from the rod tip. The lure should be allowed to sink to the bottom then it should be lifted and lowered by light jerks of the rod tip. This will cause the Nobbler to dance seductively in the centre of the trout's chosen territory. Usually the fish launches an immediate assault on the lure, an attack that normally proves fatal.

The fascinating aspect of this style of fishing is that every movement of the attacking fish can be seen clearly. This technique can also be used to catch trout which have taken up position under a raft of floating debris. Most fisheries contain rafts of this type, made up of weed, leaves, cut rushes and twigs, and when welded together by wind action these rafts provide a perfect stronghold for large trout.

By flicking the Nobbler into the water at the very edge of the raft, it is often possible to get an instant strike from larger than average fish.

In this sort of situation timing the strike is seldom easy. The fish is impossible to see until the very second it strikes the lure. I remember one such fish at Damerham in Hampshire which actually made nine strikes at the lure before I finally hooked it! This fish – a near five pound rainbow, in perfect condition – came so fast that on each occasion I struck too soon or too late and pulled the lure from its mouth.

Initially I had started fishing with an all-yellow nobbler. As the fish wised up, I changed to white and it ultimately fell to a black version. I am convinced that under such conditions regular colour changes are essential. Once a fish becomes wary of one colour the clever angler will switch to another, often meeting with instant success as a direct result.

Trout can be stalked where the water is clear. The author landing a fine Damerham rainbow.

Author with Nythe limit, including three 'double-figure' fish.

Personal Victories

Since designing the Dog Nobbler I have caught many outstanding trout. I am convinced that many of these fish would have eluded me had I not used the Nobbler. In one season alone I caught twenty double-figure rainbow trout, including one of over 16 pounds. My best brown trout to date took a yellow Dog Nobbler and weighed in at nearly 7½ pounds.

On several occasions I have taken more than one double-figure rainbow trout on the same day. I remember a particularly successful occasion in Hampshire at Nythe Lake near Alresford. Conditions looked poor on arrival at the lake. Mid April is notoriously blustery, and heavy storm clouds constantly threatened rain and sleet. To make things even more difficult, an icy wind of near gale force was whipping the surface of the small lake to foam. Hardly trout fishing weather.

Despite the terrible conditions I made a start, taking a near 5 pound fish on the second or third cast. Nearly an hour later, I hadn't touched another fish and was just beginning to think of going up to the fishing hut for coffee when directly behind the incoming fly I saw a broad flash as a big fish turned away. Hastily making another cast my perseverance was rewarded by a heavy take from an obviously large trout.

Some large trout show little inclination to fight. This one was different. From the moment it felt the hook, the fish started to run directly back down the lake to a thick central weed bed. This was one of the few trout I have caught which took not only all the fly line but half the backing line as well. Each time I brought the big fish back to within netting range it turned and began to run. Finally, however, it was in the net and back at the hut it weighed in at 12¾ pounds. Knowing the ways of large trout, I returned to the same casting position and within minutes had an 11 pounder in the net.

Strange as it may seem I have often caught big fish in poor climatic conditions. On one occasion I fished as a guest on the famed Willow Pool at Linch Hill Fishery, Oxford. Conditions were really appalling, with a driving rain and a force 10 wind to make life virtually unbearable. I had come to fish, however, and fish I would.

Willow Pool is a large and expensive water, stocked with

nothing but large fish. Five pounds is the average weight although fish up to and over ten pounds can be expected.

On arrival, I found three other anglers already fishing, but none had touched or even seen a trout. Trout of all sizes, move into the wind and then gather in the depths when reaching the bank. Taking this into consideration, I chose to fish almost directly into the wind from the north side of the lake.

The water in this area was murky with suspended silt and its murkiness influenced my choice of fly colour. If anything would catch trout there it would be a yellow Dog Nobbler. Casting was difficult, due to the wind's strength. Even so, by casting down and across a small, rather deep bay I was able to work out a fair length of line: enough, in fact, to catch fish.

In less than an hour I took four magnificent rainbow trout. Three of them over 7 pounds in weight and one of 5 pounds 5 ounces. All took yellow Dog Nobblers, fished deep and fast on a fast sinking, forward taper line. This line – supplied to me by ace British trout angler Bob Church – has the weight to sink fast and has proved perfect for fishing the Nobbler.

Tying the Dog Nobbler

Standard Nobbler

Take a size 8 long shank hook and – with a pair of small round-nose pliers, or small forceps – grip the hook behind the eye and bend gently downwards to offset the hook for about three-sixteenths of an inch along the shank behind the eye, at an angle of about 40 degrees (see Figure 12).

Next, take some lead wire (I use a medium gauge) and wind on the wire neatly, from the top of the 'offset' to in front of the eye. Make sure that you leave plenty of room behind the eye to finish off the head easily, six or seven turns of the lead is about right. I usually put a spot or two of varnish on the lead coils, and then bind down with tying silk.

Once this has been completed, the lure can be tied. For the tail tie in a bunch of marabou equal in length to that of the hook: experience will show how much to use, though I feel it is better to underdo than overdo it.

Next, tie in at the tail a piece of chenille, and silver wire/tinsel or similar, and wind the chenille up the shank of the lure to the lead. Put a little varnish on the shank to help hold down the body material. Then form a body with the chenille that thickens towards the head. Take it right up to the lead coils on the 'offset', tie in and trim off the excess. Then wind the wire up the body in the opposite direction and cut off at the head. Trim the body as necessary.

Colours And Variations

The Dog Nobbler is effective in a variety of colours . . . white, black, olive, orange, and yellow being the most popular. One colour is very often more successful than others at certain times of the day, so it pays to vary your choice through the day.

One small variation that does quite well at times, is to give the Nobbler a body hackle. The Nobbler is tied in the usual way but a feather is tied in at the tail and wound up the body and fixed down with the wire tinsel.

Mayfly Nobbler

For the tail, use white marabou plus four or five strands of pheasant tail tied over the marabou but of about a third of its length.

The body is made up of four or five strands of white ostrich herl twisted into a rope, plus three strands of pheasant tail also twisted into a rope. Tie in white ostrich, then brown pheasant tail, make two turns with the white – hold with tying silk – and make half turns with brown, making a small brown band.

Next, two or thee turns of white, then two or three turns of brown and then back to white. Trim off brown at this point, and make the rest of the body with white. Tie off at lead coils and trim the body of long flue.

The result should be a velvet body, with two clear brown rings at its base. Finish as for the normal Nobbler using bronze peacock herl or brown marabou silk.

To develop the pattern a little further use the Walker Nymph dressing, which is as follows:

Take a small bunch of pheasant tail herls and tie in by the butts, three-quarters along the body; with pints facing toward tail. Form a thorax with white ostrich herl (three strands), tie down but do not trim. Bring pheasant tail forward over thorax to form wing case. Divide the tips into two and tie either side of the thorax. Form head with silk then varnish head.

Seven good rainbows from Damerham, weighing 38½ pounds in all.

Reservoir Style

Reservoir trout fishing is a highly popular sport, calling for adapted techniques and, where possible, an intimate knowledge of the reservoir's contours.

Contrary to popular belief most reservoirs are not simply gigantic concrete bowls. In many cases the reservoir has been created by flooding whole valleys, trees, houses, and streams, which have all disappeared under the water. It is these sort of hidden features that a reservoir angler should know about if he or she hopes to catch fish consistently.

To give an idea of the magnitude of the problem of knowing what is where, it is only necessary to consider the vast size of many of the British trout reservoirs. Grafham Water, for example, covers 1,600 acres, while Rutland Water spreads over 3,200 acres but is still small in comparison to Kielder.

When faced with such large areas the first problem is finding the trout. Not only might they be concentrated in a fairly small area, they may also be feeding at any point between the very deep bottom and the surface.

Weather conditions are another major factor in reservoir fishing: if the wind has been blowing in one direction for several days, then it is safe to assume that many of the trout will have congregated on the windward bank; and if the day is cloudy and overcast, then fish are far more likely to feed at the surface than if the day is bright.

Methods

When boat fishing it is best to use a rudder or drift controller, if the reservoir rules allow. The method then is to set the rudder so that the boat drifts along the bank, and to cast at right angles to the boat.

Fishing this is simple: using a sinking line first allow your line to sink and when it has been pulled through an arc and is trailing straight behind the boat, begin to retrieve your fly. Savage takes often occur just as the fly speeds up, as it passes through the bend of the arc.

On reservoirs where rudders are not allowed by the authorities, the rate of drift can be controlled by a drogue, which is of similar shape to a parachute and is hung in the water behind the boat, where it slows down the drift. Similar tactics are used with the drogue as with the rudder. Both of these methods allow an angler to cover a great deal of water.

If trout are not located within a reasonable space of time, it is advisable to change lines, to fish at a different depth. This is achieved by using either a slower or faster sinking line, or counting off and allowing more or less time for the fly to sink.

Using A Floating Line

Where fish can be seen rising or boiling just under the surface, it is obviously sensible to use a floating line and a team of nymphs or wet flies. These are fished very slowly, across the wind with no movement whatsoever except the movement given by the drift of the boat.

Fish moving up into the wind are often very easy to take on this method. However, if the wind is too strong, and the boat is drifting fast, it is advisable to anchor in an area where trout have been sighted and fish across the wind. Once again, the flies should be allowed to drift, although an occasional twitch on the line may tempt a trout to strike.

Recommended flies for reservoir fishing from a boat are the Leopard Nymph, Buzzers, Black and Peacock Spider, Sedge pupa, Pheasant Tail or the more traditional choice of March Brown, Butcher, Dunkeld and Invicta. Most nymphs can be used as well, but these flies usually catch well in most conditions.

Drift fishing is often pointless when the trout are concentrated in a small area. The best plan then is to anchor, to take full advantage of the hot spot. On these occasions you will find that a small lure worked slowly through the water, works well. In a case like this, flies such as the Appetizer, Dog Nobbler, Church Fry, Whisky Fly, Jack Frost, Marabou and Sweeney Todd are all very effective.

If boats are unavailable and you are restricted to bank fishing, make for the windward bank and, if the bank is indented, then that is even better, for by taking up a position on the point of a bay it is possible to cast directly across the wind with a team of nymphs or wet flies, which are then allowed to swing round exactly in the manner described for boat fishing.

Where the water is deep, a sinking line should be used. This will enable you to retrieve slowly without snagging the bottom although, at a pinch, a floating line coupled with a long leader can also be employed. Use the same flies as you would when boat fishing.

To get the best out of bank fishing on a reservoir it pays to move until a hot spot is located. When the wind is blowing directly onto the bank, the trout often move to take advantage of food dislodged from the bottom by the water's wave action, for in shallow water the bottom is stirred up, which readily attracts feeding fish. If you fail to catch trout then change depths and speed of retrieve until you locate the fish.

Reservoirs – My Choice

Of the many reservoirs in England, Rutland Water is certainly the best known and a mecca for the fly angler. The fish there are growing rapidly, they fight well and have a good average size.

Grafham is also still a good venue while Keilder seems to be a strong future contender but, as yet, is still a comparatively new water.

Chew and Blagdon are long established and hold some fine fish although they are both moody waters. However, they produce well when conditions are right.

Ravensthorpe is small but pretty, and some big fish have been caught there in the past although, sadly, good fish are now rare.

Other reservoirs to recommend are Ardleigh and Hanningfield, while Welsh and West Country reservoirs provide good, often low-cost fishing.

Wimbleball, Siblyback and Sutton Bingham make perfect 'away day' waters and all can provide first class sport: Wimbleball also holds some fine tiger trout.

A 5½ pound rainbow for fly-tier Roy Buckland, taken from Rooksbury Mill Trout Fishery, near Andover in Hampshire.

A 9 pound brownie in superb
condition, from Nythe Lake,
Alresford in Hampshire *(left)*.

Netting a good $12\frac{3}{4}$ pound
rainbow at Nythe Lake *(above)*.

Double limit for Roy Buckland
and the author at Rooksbury Mill
(right).

Top lures: Muddlers, Copper Nymph, Mayfly Nymph and green Baby Doll *(above left)*.

Fishing the evening rise on the famous River Test *(left)*.

Good 11 pound 6 ounce rainbow, taken on a Dog Nobbler *(above)*.

Fly fishing for trout on the Test
carrier stream at the Broadlands
Estate near Romsey *(left)*.

Fishing in the New Forest,
Hampshire. Leo Jarmal's
Leominstead Trout Fishery *(top)*.

Playing a rainbow at
Hucklesbrook Trout Lakes near
Fordingbridge *(above)*.

Trout from the River Test carrier at Broadlands *(above left)*.
Sea trout angler on the Lymington River in Hampshire *(left)*.
Author with 5 pound rainbow from Rooksbury Mill *(above)*.

Playing out an over-wintered 5 pound 8 ounce brownie from a lake at Whitesheet Farm in Dorset, taken on a green Dog Nobbler *(above)*.

River Test brownie in very good condition *(left)*.

Author and fisherman/author Peter Wheat with $12\frac{1}{2}$ and $11\frac{1}{2}$ pound rainbows respectively, taken during the Izaak Walton Tercentenary celebrations *(above right)*.

Test brownie on a small green nymph *(right)*.

Good tiger trout (left) and a
rainbow from Bossington Lake,
Hampshire *(left)*.

Author with beautifully-
conditioned 4 pound 4 ounce tiger
trout from Nythe Lake *(above)*.

Tigers like orange. This one was
taken on a Dog Nobbler *(right)*.

Des Strange with a 9 pound 6
ounce rainbow in perfect
condition, from Leominstead
Trout Fishery *(above left)*.

Beautiful 'triploid' weighing $5\frac{1}{2}$
pounds. Taken at Waterways
Trout Fishery near Warminster in
Wiltshire *(left)*.

Author with two 9 and one $8\frac{3}{4}$
pound trout from the Test carrier
stream at Broadlands *(above)*.

Browns love black *(right)*.

Good fish from Nythe Lake on a
stormy day *(above left)*.

Author with 5 pound fish from
Whitesheet Farm, Dorset *(far left)*.

Flies before Housby got to them
(left).

A 5 pound 4 ounce brownie from
Whitesheet Farm *(above)*.

Dry fly fishing on the River Ebble
near Salisbury in Wiltshire *(right)*.

Roy Mason and friends with a good bag from Leominstead in the New Forest *(above)*.

Head of a 7 pound golden rainbow from Leominstead *(left)*.

Good brownie taken on a Dog Nobbler *(right)*.

Fishing on the Test feeder stream at the Broadlands Estate *(far left)*.

Author with a good bag of triploids from Waterways Trout Fishery near Warminster, all taken on nymph *(above left)*.

Author with 7 pound rainbow from Linch Hill Trout Fishery, Oxfordshire *(above)*.

A 5 pound 4 ounce tiger trout taken from Nythe Lake on a Dog Nobbler *(left)*.

A beautiful brownie taken on a Shrimpfly, Orkney *(left)*.

Well back from the water. Dryfly fishing on a chalk stream *(top)*.

The first Dog Nobblers, yellow with marabou and blue with ostrich *(above)*.

Brown, rainbow and two brook trout *(above right)*.

Evening over Hundland Loch, Orkney *(overleaf)*.

Rainbow Trout

The rainbow trout, *salmo gairdneri,* is a native of the Pacific coast, rivers and lakes of the North American continent, ranging from the Bering Sea in the north to the coast of Southern California in the south. It was introduced into Britain late last century, has rarely bred successfully in the wild and, in most cases, exists now only as a result of continual restocking by fish farms which have bred the species successfully by modern stripping techniques.

I believe that rainbow trout breed naturally in the Derbyshire Wye and the Chess. I understand, however, that this natural breeding of stocked fish is now on the decline.

Rainbows are highly suitable for introduction to reservoirs and other stillwaters because they live for only four to five seasons, and can be stocked in various sizes. Under most farming conditions, a one-year-old fish will be between 4 and 10 inches, attaining between 6 and 12 inches in its second year, while a third year fish will be between 14 and 22 inches.

These are average figures and can be exceeded with suitable feeding and good water conditions. Only a few years ago a 10 pound rainbow was exceptional, now fish of this size are comparatively common.

Far hardier a fish than the brown trout, the rainbow can withstand high water temperatures, low oxygen levels and cloudy water: the three things fatal to a brown. It is also a far more active fish, being a free riser to the fly and often living and moving in small shoals. The rainbow is very similar in appearance to the brown trout, apart from a distinctive wide lateral band of iridescent red/purple along the flanks. It is

FIGURE 14   A male rainbow trout.

usually black spotted, and these spots – unlike those of the brown – grow on the fins and tail.

Rainbow trout grow faster and to a larger maximum size than brown trout. They also spawn later than brown trout and are therefore in excellent condition on British waters to the very end of the season, although during the early days of the next season 'black' rainbows (late spawners) may be encountered.

Rainbows feed on a very similar diet to brown trout. When young they exist on daphnia and other infusoria but, once past the fry stage, they quickly graduate to feeding on shrimp and insects and then on to snail and fish fry. Rainbow trout are more likely to rise than brown and are far more active in their search for food, ranging freely between the bottom and surface, taking full advantage of midges, nymphs, mayflies and their larvae. And in waters where the fry of coarse fish are plentiful, rainbows soon become dedicated fry feeders.

It is not unusual for anglers to find small rainbows stuffed full of coarse fish fry, for rainbows become almost as predatory as pike and, as rainbows move in loose shoals, they are sometimes seen driving shoals of small roach, rudd or perch ahead of them.

Rainbows often rise freely in blustery weather, feeding well on the surface during high winds. They will often cruise upwind in such conditions, dropping into the depths when they come to the shore line.

Dry Fly Fishing

In calmer weather, when the surface is like a millpond, rainbows will often rise to midges and other tiny flies on the surface, totally ignoring all the wet flies and lures offered by fishermen and under these circumstances, a dry fly is often highly successful.

Rainbows usually move fast when they hit a dry fly. 'Smash takes' occur in these conditions, even when the leader is heavy. I find that once rising, rainbows are not too selective about fly patterns, as long as the fly is similar in colour to the natural hatch.

Good sized rainbow from Leominstead showing standard rainbow
markings.

Wet Fly/Lure Fishing

Under average conditions, with a light breeze on the water, rainbows feed well. The broken surface of the water also prevents fish from spotting an angler's movements too easily, as well as covering up the angler's mistakes when working the fly. Under these conditions, the traditional wet fly method is a fine system to employ, both from the bank or from a boat.

A team of three wet flies can be used with a long cast which, fished slowly, presents them at different levels, often enabling the angler to locate the best depth. Medium casting from the bank, or short lining from a boat can also be very productive.

When rainbows are down deep and disinclined to show themselves, the angler must fish the water, covering as much ground as he or she can, to get fish moving or to locate moving fish. Under these conditions, a lure is usually ideal, the Dog Nobbler being particularly successful. If this fly fails then other patterns should be tried at various depths and different speeds.

The angler will often have to scratch bottom to find fish. This is best achieved with a leaded lure, fished slow.

Rainbows can often be tempted when high water temperatures have caused brown trout to go off feeding completely. They will also move quite fast from comparatively deep water to a tempting fly, if it is fished realistically on or near the surface, following it until it is about to break surface, for many good fish are taken in the last seconds of a cast.

When a buzzer rise occurs in the evening, fish may become preoccupied with nymphing. This makes for exciting fishing. When fish are hooked high in the water they will often leap and splash on the surface.

My Methods

During the past decade I have caught many double-figure rainbow trout, including fish of 16 pounds 2 ounces, 14 pounds 2 ounces and 13 pounds 12 ounces. All these fish have been caught from stillwater fisheries. I have yet to catch a ten pound rainbow from running water as far as river fisheries are

Playing a rainbow at Leominstead.

concerned, although in the days when I had a rod on the Test carrier trout stream at Broadlands, near Romsey in Hampshire, I managed to catch three huge rainbows in a single day's fishing.

The day in question was hot, its bright sunshine and clear blue sky making it far from perfect for trout fishing. It was obviously a day when the fish would stay deep, using the streamer weed as protection. In short, a day when catches would probably be on the low side.

Taking all these facts into consideration I decided to walk the upstream section of Number One Beat, in the hope of spotting a fish I could cast to. My partner, Bryn Hammond, decided to adopt similar tactics for the lower section of the beat. Starting off upstream I walked slowly along, keeping well back from the river.

Twice in the first 100 yards I saw fish but both were too small to try for. Then, about halfway up the beat, I caught sight of a huge tail protruding from beneath a bank of streamer weed. Standing still I allowed my eyes to become totally adjusted to the water reflections, and soon I was able to make out a long thick-bodied trout, lying in a near perfect position below the throat of the pool. The stream at this point was a little over four feet deep.

As I watched I could see the great rainbow move forward to intercept some form of food too small for me to see. My problem then was to find a position from which I could cast to the trout, and to find a fly colour that would tempt it to feed. Upstream casting was out of the question, the streamer weed would have blanketed the fly long before it could sink to fish level, but by taking an upstream position and fishing down to the trout I was able to get a fly down to within inches of its broad face. My initial choice was a green Damselfly Nymph, tied for me by Roy Buckland. This obviously resembled the natural nymphs being taken by the trout for, as my nymph swept towards its position, the fish eased out and swung across to intercept it.

At this point I was certain the fish would take; unfortunately, it changed its mind and eased back under the waving weed. Twice more the fish came out to look at my nymph, but then it stopped showing interest and changing patterns brought absolutely no further response from the trout.

71

Netting a good rainbow.

At the same time, the fish was not in anyway 'spooked' for it continued to feed in a most obvious way, its iron jaw opening and closing repeatedly.

By now I was determined to catch that fish. The trout had showed initial interest in my damsel nymph so I switched back to this pattern, double checking the knot as I tied the nymph to the cast.

My plan was to make a maximum of three casts, then rest the fish for a ten minute spell. Flogging the water was out. I was sure the trout was unaware of my presence but I had no intention of alarming it by too much bankside activity, which meant giving the great rainbow a rest from my efforts. In all, it was exactly two hours before the fish decided to take my fly.

Bryn Hammond having exhausted the lower section of the beat had, by this time, worked his way up and was fishing less than 50 yards downstream from my position. In fairness, he had no idea of my whereabouts and I was in no position to stand up and reveal where I was! Then – just as I thought Bryn would wander up and frighten the monster – the trout moved forward, opened its huge white mouth and sucked in the nymph.

I struck and the second I did so the big trout took off at high speed. It turned downstream at first but, as soon as it entered the shallows at the tail of the pool, it panicked, turned at speed and swept up and out of the pool dragging a great bag of line behind it.

Hearing the scream of my reel, Bryn Hammond arrived just in time to see the great fish leave the pool. Later he told me he could hardly believe the size of the trout. Being the good angler he is, he promptly snapped open my big landing net and stood back to give me room to play the fish out.

My biggest headache was a jumble of sunken alder roots which the trout had earmarked as its means of escape. Time and again it tried to bulldoze its way into the tangle, and each time I managed to turn it away.

Finally, after nearly 15 minutes of continuous action, the fish turned on its side and Bryn moved in with the net. Totally spent, the trout slid over the net rim and into the bag of the net. Having killed it quickly with the priest, I carried it back to the fish hut where it weighed in at exactly nine pounds. A beautiful fish, in near perfect condition.

With three fish still to go I wandered off upstream, hoping to sight a few reasonable trout before I arrived at the weir pool at the top of the beat. Unfortunately I didn't see a single one so on arrival at the weir I followed my customary habit of walking up onto the brickwork of the weir, directly above the inflow culvert. Here I could sit and look down into ten feet of clear water, where with luck I would see some trout activity.

Initially I saw very little, then I saw a broad flash as a big fish rolled almost directly below me. A few minutes later the flash was repeated, and this time I saw yet another huge trout which was patrolling the pool, pause to roll its side on a sunken projection below my feet. Watching closely, I saw the fish repeat the process time and again.

Casting from the top of the wall was impossible so I tied on a heavy fluorescent green nymph and flicked it out a little more than leader length, so that it sank down close to the sunken obstruction. My eyes were now accustomed to the water and I clearly saw the trout heading towards it scratching post. As it rolled, I lifted the bright nymph into its path and the fish took it instantly. Setting the hook was simple as I was directly above the trout but the resulting battle was not so easy. The big fish went totally crazy, jumping and crashing about the pool in a frenzy that had to be seen to be believed, until after a number of heart-stopping incidents, it was ready for netting.

At this stage I realised just what an impossible position I was in. Even with my landing-net handle fully extended I could not reach far enough to net the fish, nor could I move off the water. I was forced, in the end, to put my faith in the crumbling brickwork and the tangle of ivy that appeared to hold the wall in place. Fortunately, everything held as I climbed down and I was able to get the fish in the net, heave it up onto the wall above and shin back to safety. That fish weighed 8¾ pounds.

Later in the afternoon I decided to walk the river with Bryn Hammond who, at this stage, was still fishless. Almost immediately we sighted yet another huge fish. Hoping that this one would fall to Bryn's rod I walked away leaving him to try his skill.

My intention was to stand and watch from a safe distance and hopefully lend a hand should the net be required. However, I still had my rod in hand, the nymph snuggled in to the keeper ring when, glancing idly at the river in front of me, I realised that I was looking straight at another large trout.

This fish was obviously feeding, I could see its mouth open and close as it moved back and forth across the current to intercept passing fly life and the opportunity was too good to miss.

My first cast dropped the nymph a yard or two ahead of the trout and as it sank the fish moved easily up to take the fly. Instantly the fish was off, causing the reel to spin and the ratchet to scream a warning to poor Bryn. Ten minutes later the fish was in the net. Sadly Bryn's hoped-for monster had vanished. My third fish weighed in at 9 pounds. Three fish, weighing just ounces under 27 pounds, was an unheard of bag of rainbows and my best brace and a half ever.

Large rainbow trout were still something of a rarity in those days and, for Broadlands trout stream, the catch was quite unbelievable. Admittedly the stream normally produced good fish but those three were exceptional. To this day they

Author with spectacular 14 pound rainbow from Avington.

Roy Hopkins and author with the record breaking Avington fish of 19
pounds 6 ounces, 'taken' and lost by Trevor earlier that day. The
author holds a 14 pound 2 ounce rainbow.

constitute my best catch of big trout from fast water.

Many 'put and take' fisheries have adopted the policy of
including the occasional monster rainbow trout among their
standard stock fish. The most notable example of this is
without doubt Avington Trout Lakes near Winchester. This
fishery has produced enormous quantities of double-figure
fish, including several record breaking specimens.

Strangely enough I have only fished at Avington on one
occasion. The day in question fell in mid April and the
weather was cold and overcast. On arrival at the fishery my
companion John Cooper and I set up our tackle and began
fishing half way along the eastern bank of the first lake. The
water was cold and extremely clear, giving me an excellent
view of the lake bed.

Opposite my position, and some twenty yards offshore, lay
a thick bank of dark green weed. It was close to this weed that
I sighted a huge trout. For early season fishing on a new water

– new to me, that is – I am inclined to fish a weighted golden shrimp. All trout like to eat shrimps and I find that if fish are on the move a shrimp retrieved in short sharp jerks will usually produce some reaction.

On my third cast a monster shadow moved out of the weed and began to trail my shrimp fly. Halfway back towards the bank the fish lost interest and retreated to the weed bed, but two casts later it came out again. This time it was obviously chasing the fly. With the trout in hot pursuit, I speeded up my rate of retrieve, causing the shrimp to dance rapidly over the lake bed. Then, with only yards to go, the vast rainbow shot forward and engulfed the shrimp. I had never seen a trout as big as that one. The strange thing was I knew as I struck that I was going to miss.

Sure enough, as I struck, the fish opened its vast mouth and the fly shot out. For a split second neither of us moved and in that time, I was able to see a distinctive white mark on its shoulder. Then it turned and fled towards the weed bed.

For an hour I saw no sign of another fish until I noticed a flicker of fins close to the weed bed and on the next cast a nice fish cruised out and sipped in the shrimp. With the fish well hooked, I settled back to enjoy the battle. The rainbow, which looked about eight pounds, was a fast fish given to spectacular aerobatics. Finally, however, I was able to wear it down ready for netting.

The Avington rule is that an angler must net his or her own fish and, at this stage, the fish still looked to weigh around eight pounds. As the fish slid into the net, however, it turned on its side to reveal a huge flank and I realised for the first time that this was no ordinary specimen. Dropping the rod I used two hands to heave the fish ashore in the net and within minutes I was back at the house, watching the official scales swing round to indicate 14 pounds 2 ounces.

Naturally I could hardly believe my luck but – on my way back to the lake – I started to wonder to myself how big that first lost fish would have been. I soon found out for in the early afternoon Swindon angler Roy Hopkins set his hook into a fish which fought for over 1½ hours. The fight ranged over half the lake, finally culminating in an exhausted angler dragging a huge trout ashore. That fish weighed in at 19 pounds 6 ounces and on its back was the distinctive white mark.

Two lovely 15 pounders from Nythe.

Without question, Roy's monster was my lost trout. At the time that fish became the record but it was a record which stood for only two short days.

The best trout I ever caught was my 16 pound 2 ounce fish taken on the very first day of a newly opened lake. The lake was still in its raw state and on the day in question it did not look particularly pretty. The water, however, was as clear as glass with only a few wisps of weed protruding from the lake bed.

I started fishing at about ten in the morning and by ten-thirty I had caught 2 fine four-pound rainbow trout. I was using an early version of my Dog Nobbler fly, still comparatively crude but, none the less, effective. As always, trout were slamming in to the fly at high speed so, when I received a very gentle take I assumed, quite wrongly, that a small fish was responsible.

To make matters worse, the trout did not at first show much temper or strength. Instead it trailed slowly along, convincing me that I had hooked a tiny fish. Imagine my feelings when a huge trout suddenly surfaced directly in front of my position, my bright Dog Nobbler jutting from its jaw.

Fortunately for me I had the presence of mind to release line as the fish took off on its first long run. This was one of the few trout I have hooked that took out all my fly line and a fair length of my backing as well. Large trout normally fight hard but close in, this fish was different. Its obvious intention was to put as much distance between us as possible and, initially, I was content to let it go. The only danger was that it might make a wide circle round a central island but even then, the level bank would give me a chance to follow it round.

With approximately 50 yards of line out, the fish turned and came at speed down the lake. It ran so fast that my line left a visible wake across the lake surface. At the end of its run it surfaced, not in a clean jump but in a flurry of tail-smacking temper that left the water foaming. I always worry when trout do this that the hook will fall out for I have seen many a big trout lost during such a flurry, and if ever I wanted a fish on the bank it was this one. The hook hold held, however, and the fish decided to surge off on another long run.

Where possible, I always prefer to play fish with the line through my fingers rather than with the reel. Anglers who insist on winding up slack line usually end up losing their fish, as the continuous action of tightening and slackening a line soon loosens even the firmest hook hold. By playing a fish on the line and using the fingers of your reel hand as a brake a fish can be kept on a taut line at all times.

This fish was still strong and its run down the lake was at high speed. For a second time I felt the join of my backing line jolt through my fingers and – to avoid losing backing – I started to follow that fish along the bank. By now most of the other anglers on the lake had stopped fishing to watch the battle and, as I gained on the still-running fish, one of the watchers picked up my big landing net and came to stand beside me. Unless I know another angler's experience and ability with a net I prefer to net my own fish. Even so, I was pleased that he had enough sense and forethought to bring the net to me.

The fish slowed down and started to jag its great body from side to side. This is typical 'fight style' for all large rainbows. And this one actually rolled over at times, to reveal its white belly. I knew then that the fish was about finished so I increased rod pressure and started to bring it in to the bank. Netting was little more than a formality as it was now totally exhausted. That fish is probably the largest rainbow trout I shall ever have the good fortune to catch.

Brown Trout

The brown trout, *salmo trutta,* is indigenous to Europe, north
west Asia and North Africa. The sea trout is a migratory form
which, like the salmon, spends much of its life in the sea,
returning to the river of its birth as it becomes ready to spawn.
Once it has spawned, it makes its way back to the sea until the
next spawning season. The brown trout is the non-migratory
form, which lives in rivers and lakes.

There are several distinct variations of brown trout which
appear in particular locations. Once considered to be separate,
distinct species (or at least sub-species), these fish were even
given scientific names to distinguish their specific status. More
recently they were shown to be capable of interbreeding, and
are now regarded as variable members of the same species,
known universally as *salmo trutta.* However, local names persist
with continued reference to the gilaroo trout of the Irish loughs
or the famed Loch Leven trout.

Brown trout are to be found in many river systems. They
normally live in the swifter rivers or streams, where the rocky,
gravelly or stony bottoms and a swift flow produces the high
oxygen requirement they need to survive and reproduce. The
slower rivers which produce good coarse fishing seldom fish
well for trout, although the odd brown trout may occur,
usually by way of a side stream where conditions and habitat
are more suitable to their needs.

Brown trout in Britain are very much a fish either of
moorland streams or traditional chalk streams of Southern

FIGURE 15   A male brown trout.

England. However, they also live well in lakes, reservoirs and ponds if conditions are suitable and intensive restocking programmes have led to a total redistribution of the species throughout Britain. Many fine new waters have appeared in regions such as the South East and the Midlands where few suitable rivers remained for trout.

Waters rich in calcium stimulate the growth of insects, molluscs and freshwater shrimps. In such waters the generous food supplies favour big, fast growing fish. Blagdon and Chew reservoirs are notable examples of food-rich waters, where introduced brown trout revert to the wild state and grow on to reach weights of 6 or even 7 pounds. The chalk streams of the south also produce excellent fish. The Rivers Avon, Kennet, Test and Itchen are typical examples. In Ireland many loughs are well known for their high quality of fish. Less favoured waters, like the tiny becks and streams of some northern and western districts, produce small, mature but game brown trout which seldom reach weights of more than 4 to 6 ounces but provide excellent sport on light lines.

Brown trout spawn at somewhere between two and four years of age. The incubation period is variable and scientific research indicates that the time varies according to water temperatures. In the wild state this ranges from 21 weeks at 2°C (36°F) to four weeks at 12°C (54°F). Losses are high during this incubation period. And out of 10,000 eggs produced it is possible that only about 260 fish survive to the end of the first year.

Growth rates vary too. Depending on the water quality and availability of food, a year old fish may be anything between 4 and 13 inches. Most brown trout obtain the majority of their food from or near the bottom. They supplement this basic diet with water-borne flies, and insects living in or on the surface. They are not fussy about what they eat when they are hungry, and will snap up almost anything which moves provided they can manage to swallow it.

In rivers, the fish tend to select a territorial base or 'lie' which is protected from the full force of the current: each fish has its own territory, and the current brings food supplies regularly. River trout surface feed far more than their reservoir counterparts.

A really good 'lie' never remains untenanted; as soon as one fish is caught a second will move in to take advantage of the regular food supply. Every angler knows the hot spots in his own river, and can often stalk a known fish in a known lie.

The reservoir angler often has the advantage of coloured water. Here fish rise less often but nevertheless patrol their territories, usually giving away their rising spots. Reservoir and lake territories are larger and may be vacated occasionally, as the fish cruise up the wind lanes or around the margins in their search for food.

My Methods

Every angler has to start somewhere. For me my trout fishing began as a child in East Devon, fishing a tiny steam called the River Love which runs through the lovely village of Luppit. This stream ultimately flows into the River Otter, a noted trout stream.

At Luppit, however, the River Love is a typical neglected West Country stream. It still holds a good head of native brown trout. 'Four to the pound' trout which fight far harder than any stew bred fish but, unfortunately, now hold little interest to the modern trout angler who thinks only in terms of giant rainbows and great stock brownies.

Periodically when the mood takes me I drive down from my Hampshire, New Forest home to wet a line in that tiny river where my obsession to fish first began. I usually go in the spring, when the primroses are out and gold kingcups glow in the watermeadows. It is a time when curlew use the valley for nesting and buzzards cruise the thermal waves on their broad flat wings.

My visits there are a sort of pilgrimage: a sad yet joyful excursion back to a time and place that only really lives in my memory of childhood. Wet boots, worms, crude fishing tackle are all a thing of the past for me but I can still remember each and every bend, and the pool where I once caught a three-quarter pound trout which, to my childish eye, was the largest fish in the world.

Now I fish the stream with a tiny brook rod, light line and a very fine leader. I always wonder if the fish will be there, and each time I cast I make an angler's prayer as my fly drops into fast water that runs slightly whisky-coloured over the pebbles. Usually I am lucky – the river likes me and I love it – and I seldom leave without taking half a dozen beautiful crimson-spotted Devon brown trout. Tiny they may be, but they are the stuff dreams are built on.

No matter where I fish, nor how large are the trout I catch, those 'four to the pound' Luppit browns still work their magic spell for me; even now, when I have fished great fly-fishing rivers like the Test.

Above a cattle bridge, directly beneath a trailing willow tree, this river ran deep over a gravel bottom which, at one point, humped up to make a raised barrier behind which I could clearly see the outline of a large trout. It could only be a brown, for on this beat on the upper reaches of the Test rainbow trout have never been stocked and are generally regarded as little more than vermin.

The fish was big, certainly in excess of six pounds. And by the movement of its broad tail and the way it occasionally left its lie it was obviously feeding: but what on? There was little or no fly on the surface, and no indication of a hatch.

Nymph fishing was allowed on the water and – under the circumstances – the best method to use. My problem was to choose the right nymph, for I knew that I would only have a couple of casts before the fish bolted upstream. So I had to get my fly selection right on the first instance. In my mind I had probably three choices: Copper Nymph, Damselfly Nymph or a particularly effective shell backed Shrimp pattern. All were known fish catchers on that particular river beat and each was worth a try.

Taking into account time of year and the light colour of the river bed, I chose to fish the Copper Nymph. My reasons were simple: being dark, this nymph would show well over the light coloured bottom, while the additional flash from the copper wire body would add a certain attraction, and the size of the nymph was – I hoped – in keeping with nymphs being taken by the big trout.

Long casting was out of the question. I had the bridge at my back while, in front of me, the trailing willow looked thick and impenetrable. Flicking the fly line as high as possible behind me I made two false casts and sent the nymph on its way. Against all odds the fly dropped perfectly, less than an inch from the willow tree tangle. Sinking quickly, it sank to fish level and I sensed rather than saw the fish take my fly.

Striking was simple but what occurred next was not. The trout felt my hook and took off like an express train, not upstream as expected but straight down, past me and on under the bridge. I had two choices, break the leader or jump into the river and try to play the trout out from under the bridge span. I chose the latter. Fortunately it was a warmish day but, even so, the waist-deep water felt icy. However, from my position, I had the advantage of being able to apply direct pressure to the fish without rubbing the line or leader on the bridge supports.

Like most large trout, this fish fought in a predictable way. And, after that first long, fast run it settled down to fight a slogging battle in the deep pool below the bridge. Occasionally it would make a short but savage rush but mostly it was content to bore deep and shake its great head.

Playing a fish of any size is simply a matter of time. This fish was big and strong but I knew that, barring accidents, constant rod pressure would soon wear it down and, sure enough, within five minutes the fish was reluctantly giving ground. Twice I had it back under the bridge, twice it made a last ditch effort and gained enough line to get back to its sanctuary pool below the bridge.

Finally, however, it was wallowing slowly but surely back upstream, towards my outstretched net. To avoid accidents I brought it an inch or two upstream of my big landing net, then let the flow of the river drift it into the mesh bag. Once it was safely in the net, I threw the rod and net up on the bank and scrambled out to give the last rites. At 7¼ pounds this was my best ever river 'brownie' and I was naturally delighted with it. In absolutely pristine condition, it looked every inch of its size and initially I thought of having it 'set up'. Later I decided to have it cold smoked instead.

Catching a huge brown trout from a famous river like the Test is one thing, when it comes to taking such fish from day-ticket fisheries the problems are far greater. To begin with, a large brown trout on a hard fished, day-ticket water soon learns about anglers. Such fish become legends. Many fisheries hold those fish and, to a degree, I have made a practice of trying to catch them. Any brown trout over 5

Author with a brownie and a rainbow from Leominstead.

pounds in weight can be regarded as a big fish: yet some fisheries hold brown trout of double this weight. In vast reservoirs like Grafham or Chew Valley this is only to be expected, but on the smaller stillwater fisheries such trout are somewhat scarce. Where I live in the south of England, there are a few fisheries in Dorset and Hampshire where such fish do exist and Whitesheet Farm (Wimborne), Rooksbury Mill (Andover) and Nythe Lake (Alresford) are all fisheries capable of producing brown trout to double-figure size.

Locating these giant brownies is not difficult. Unlike rainbow trout, which tend to wander, brown trout are very territorial and the big ones usually take up residence in a given area and stay put for the duration of their life. Such fish normally give away their position by flashing at a fly or, more likely, by simply swimming slowly into view.

The problem is that once seen and located these fish are often hammered incessantly. Often they are hooked and lost, and this adds to their fear of man and their mistrust of most flies and lures. Many anglers seem proud of being smashed by a big fish, personally I do not see this as a sign of achievement.

Every angler loses the odd large trout, but to do so consistently is simply bad fishing and most are lost because the anglers will insist on using leaders that are too fragile. On fisheries where large trout are known to exist it is, in my opinion, foolhardy to use a leader with a breaking strain of less than six pounds. I occasionally use a leader of 8 pounds and often I am very glad of that extra poundage.

Time and again, however, I see anglers fishing gossamer leaders and the end product is usually a break off on the first reasonable fish that sucks in the fly. Naturally enough, a large trout with a couple of flies embedded in its jaw soon becomes very wary and this is particularly true of brown trout.

Having located a large brown trout my usual technique is to get within casting range and then do nothing for a while. This allows the fish to relax. I then choose and use a fly which I don't think the fish will have seen before. All brown trout are selective about fly coloration and, as a general rule, the darker the fly the more likely it is to tempt a brownie.

Black, brown or olive are my first colour choices. Fluorescent orange or yellow may well attract large rainbows but these colours seldom stimulate a big brown to feed and in the majority of stillwater fisheries I think brown trout feed on leech. For this reason I normally use a black, brown or dark olive Dog Nobbler. These look very leech-like in the water and if browns are inclined to feed then the dark Nobbler will usually attract them. Big brownies seldom surface feed, and I like to work the fly close to the lake bed.

My usual tackle is a 10 foot rod combined with a weight-forward no. 9 sinking line. My favourite rod is the one I designed for Bob Church's company, the Trevor Housby Dog Nobbler rod as this is a powerful two-section carbon rod capable of handling even the largest of stock brownies.

I remember one large Whitesheet brown trout that had taken up permanent residence in a deep corner of the top lake. This fish had a lie deep down beneath a thicket of water-covered bramble and willow. Like most large trout it was a creature of habit, emerging every twenty minutes or so to cruise slowly and defiantly around its selected territory. It looked to weigh over 6 pounds and at that weight it interested me a great deal.

Initially, I tried casting to it as it cruised. Twice it looked at my lure only to turn away without attempting to take the fly, it was obviously going to be a difficult fish to tempt. I tried a change of colour. The fish had shown interest in black, now I switched to dark brown. On this occasion the trout made no attempt to even inspect the fly. Brown was out, so I went back to black.

I had noticed by this time that the trout was very precise in its movements. It had a specific route which it adhered to on every occasion. Taking this into consideration, I cast the fly out to fall in the path taken by the fish. The fly was allowed to sink to the bottom where I left it static. After a wait of approximately ten minutes I saw the trout emerge from its lie and as it approached the area of the fly I started to retrieve the Nobbler fast.

My idea was to simulate the movement of a disturbed and startled leech. The ploy obviously worked, for as the black fly lurched up out of the depths the big brown turned its head and sucked the lure straight into its mouth. A second later the fish had turned and was heading at speed for the tangle of sunken branches.

Maximum pressure was essential, so I piled on every ounce

A heavy-weight brownie.

of weight possible and with less than a foot to go I managed to turn the fish out into the lake and open water. This suited me perfectly, for I was then able to play the fish out in conventional manner, eventually bringing it to the waiting net.

At 6½ pounds it was a nice brown trout. As expected, however, it had one fly firmly embedded in its jaw and the rusting remnants of a hook in its kype. Proof once again that it had been hooked at least twice by anglers' fishing tackle that was not up to scratch.

Orkney Brown Trout

Some of my finest days with brown trout have come while fishing the magnificent lochs of Orkney. By southern standards, the Orkney brownies do not reach a great size. Swanhay Loch produces fish of over 2½ pounds but, in Harray and Hundland, the average size is around 1 to 1½ pounds.

What these fish lack in size they make up for in caution, colour and fighting power. Of the main lochs on Orkney, Harray is my favourite: a vast sweep of water studded with rock-bound skerries and dense weed beds, which provide the trout with a perfect environment.

On my first trip to Orkney my prime reason for visiting these lovely Islands was to sea fish. At the end of my first week, however, high winds made sea angling impossible and I arranged to spend a day on Loch Harray. I had brought a fly outfit with me and a wallet full of south country flies, all of which my ghillie assured me would, 'Catch no fish on the Loch!' The top local fly was a Ke-He and all the locals fished loch style, using a team of three flies.

Despite local opinion, I decided to use my own tried and trusted flies, sticking to long casting and a single fly. Donald my affable ghillie obviously regarded me as totally mad (an opinion he later changed, when he discovered I had a bottle of whisky in my bag). As a ghillie he was first rate, for he knew the contours of the loch perfectly and, despite his forebodings, it was not long before my hated southern style of fishing produced a solid take from a superb 1½ pound brown trout.

Having observed a multitude of damselflies in the reed-fringed boat bay, I had decided to try a Damselfly Nymph on the Loch. This turned out to be a good choice, producing at the end of the day a splendid bag of beautiful brown trout.

On our return to the Merilister Hotel boat bay, my fish were instantly noticed by an ageing English major. This man was a regular visitor to Orkney and, as far as I could ascertain, had caught nothing for several days.

'I say old boy,' he shouted, What fly did you catch those on?'

'Damselfly Nymph', I replied.

'Eh? Spinning, hardly sporting, what,' was his comment, and with that he stamped off towards the bar, now obviously uninterested in my catch. The following morning, however, i heard him ringing Hardy's of Pall Mall, London for a dozen Damselfly Nymphs!

Some years after this I discovered an ancient, but very attractive, water-filled quarry close to Burray Village in south Roadsay (Orkney). Inquiries revealed that it contained trout but belonged to an ancient and extremely shy Orcadian farmer. Plucking up courage, I knocked on his door, explained the purpose of my visit and was told I could fish whenever I liked for £1 per day. Money to be collected on the bank.

This seemed a reasonable arrangement and I decided to start fishing immediately. I soon discovered that the quarry was a living jewel; the sort of fishery that all trout anglers dream about and few ever find.

Obviously of ancient origin, the pool was over 50 feet deep in places. Its water was gin clear and, at one end, I could see a number of fish moving close to dense beds of thick healthy weed. The trout appeared to be nymphing rather than actively taking surface flies and this prompted me to try a shell back shrimp. On new waters I always find that a shrimp pattern invariably produces some reaction from the trout.

How right I was, my first cast produced a superb brown trout weighing at a guess a fraction over 1 pound in weight. Minutes later I took a second fish of similar weight then, while casting into deep water close to a craggy granite cliff, I was taken by a fish that I never saw, let alone stopped.

Like so many big fish, this one took the fly gently, just a tiny pluck followed by a show of power I could not hope to handle.

Then it just went down and down, until it found sanctuary under a sunken ledge. I have no doubt that it was a huge brown trout, my guess being that it weighed well into double figures. Certainly I had never before and have never since hooked a trout as powerful as the quarry pool monster.

For five days I fished that lovely pool, taking and often releasing many beautiful trout. At the end of this time I still had not seen the farmer to pay my £1 per day, so back I went to knock on the farmhouse door. Once again I found myself speaking to the farmer, who looked blankly at the money I offered.

'Did ye enjoy the fishing?' He asked.

'I truly did,' I answered.

'Then ye have no need to pay,' he said, and closed the door. Typical Orcadian kindness.

Sea Trout

The sea trout is a migratory form of *salmo trutta,* found from
the Bay of Biscay north to the White Sea. It lives and spawns
in a wide variety of waters, and the idea that sea trout exist
only in the wild, fast rivers is far from accurate. In the south of
England, for example, some of the top sea trout rivers are
extremely sluggish: the Sussex Ouse being a typical example.

Sea trout are one of the shyest of all game fish. For this
reason most sea trout fishing – in normal to low water – is
done at dusk or in full darkness.

The perfect sea trout rod is single handed and about 10 feet
long. It should be capable of handling a no. 8 or 9 double-
taper or forward-taper line and the actual leader should be
slightly shorter than the rod. I normally fish a 9 or 9½ foot
leader taken directly from a spool of Maxima nylon of 8
pounds breaking strain. Tapered leaders are not necessary.
Choice of fly is up to the angler, but the old saying, 'Any
colour as long as it's black', stands as good advice when sea
trout are the quarry.

Night fishing for sea trout is a fascinating experience. The
best nights often come after a sharp but warm shower of rain,
when the sky is overcast rather than clear. Never be in a hurry
to begin fishing. Many anglers spoil their chances by fishing
while it is still light. It is far better to wait until full dark, then
cast to fish heard splashing on the water: this splashing is the
signal to start fishing.

Concentrate, at first, on the faster sections of the river and

FIGURE 16   A male sea trout.

leave the quiet glides and tails until full darkness. Make your first cast out to a point slightly downstream and across the current. Casts will have to be made in the dark, so it pays to stick some form of indicator onto the line to show the correct amount of line to use. I use a tiny tag of electrical tape.

Once a fish is hooked it will usually put on a hair-raising show of aerobatics. This can be dangerous. Fresh run sea trout have very tender mouths, and many hooked fish escape when the hook comes free during a twisting leap. The thrill of hooking and playing a spirited sea trout in the dark is a magical experience, and your catch may be anything from 1 pound to a specimen 10 pounds plus.

Hugh Falkus, king of the sea trout men, divides the night into three distinct sections, which he calls 'first-half' (before midnight), 'half-time' (up to about 1 *a.m.*) and 'second-half' (from 1 *a.m.* until dawn). These distinct periods reflect the changing habits of sea trout during the night. The trout are active at the surface during the first half, retiring to deeper water after midnight.

Falkus believes the angler should use a surface fly on a floating line during the 'first-half'. 'Half-time' is when the fish are at their most unco-operative: a time for the angler to take a rest, eat a sandwich and change the floating line for a sinking one, fishing out the 'second half' with a sunk lure. Second half fish will sometimes hit a big tandem lure that is fished deep. This type of lure, designed to simulate a small fish often produces a 'take' from the biggest of the fish in the river.

Very occasionally sea trout can be caught in daylight, often following a good flood when the water is clearing. At this point it is possible to make good catches in daytime but such chances come only rarely.

Flies for Sea Trout

The life cycle of the sea trout is almost the same as that of the salmon with one important difference, that whereas salmon do not feed in freshwater, sea trout occasionally do.

The flies to concentrate on are those that represent the sea trout's main diet while at sea; in other words small fish. Sea

96

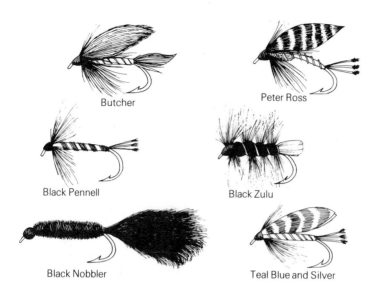

Butcher

Peter Ross

Black Pennell

Black Zulu

Black Nobbler

Teal Blue and Silver

FIGURE 17   Essential flies for sea trout. (See page 141 for patterns.)

trout also feed on prawns, shrimps, etc., but small fish constitute its main diet. Successful flies are Teal Blue and Silver, Peter Ross, Silver Wilkinson, Teal and Red, Mallard and Silver, Mallard and Gold, and other bright patterns tied to imitate small fish.

Every river or loch has its own special fly patterns but these are usually variations of the patterns mentioned above. The size of a fly is more important than its shape, and when choosing this a great deal depends upon the weather and water conditions, although standard patterns should be sizes 8 to 10 under normal conditions.

Colour is also important. Dark flies seem to catch better than light coloured flies. Other suggested patterns are Black Pennell, Black Dog Nobbler, Butcher, and Black Zulu. And if you fish a team of three flies the Black Pennell is highly successful as a tail fly. Gold or silver rigging should be used on all sea trout flies.

Whether you use a large or small fly depends mainly on the

season. In the early season you may well agree that a big fly catches more fish than a small fly, but the longer the trout stays in a river on its return from the sea, the more likely it is to return to the smaller sized food available in its new environment, such as nymphs, shrimps and flies.

Fly patterns for sea trout are legion and most were designed by over-enthusiastic fly tyers. In my opinion, only a small selection of tried and tested flies should be carried: black being the predominant colour in the selection. In the case of Dog Nobblers – which are proving to be good for sea trout – white and yellow should also be carried, while Tiger Nobblers which have, say, a yellow body and black tail can also be exceptional fish catchers.

My Methods

Sea trout can be caught from saltwater, something I had read about but never experienced until I made my first visit to Orkney in the late 1970s. At the time I was involved in producing a series of fishing brochures for the Orkney Tourist Office and one of the places I stayed was Burray Village, not far from South Ronaldsay.

Close to the village a tiny stream flowed down to enter the bay. This stream was little more than an irrigation ditch, but the flow of water was enough to attract and hold migrating sea trout. Local anglers – intent on fishing for the pot – used spinning tackle to take these fish. I decided, however, to fly fish, using a local tardan fly, which had a blue palmered body, blue wings, and a silver underwrap to add sparkle.

My rod was a 9 foot 6 inch carbon, matched to an appropriate weight-forward sinking line. I had been told that the stream mouth regularly produced good fish so to avoid breakages, I tackled up with a leader of 8 pounds breaking strain. I have never been convinced that a hunting fish is leader shy, in fact, I believe that once a fish sees the fly it centres its whole attention on that object and never even notices the actual leader.

Orkney never really gets dark during mid summer: between midnight and one in the morning a sort of bright twilight

98

occurs, and then the sun reappears. So night fishing is out of the question. For this reason I chose instead to fish the twilight hour.

Having kept an eye on the area, I had already sighted several leaping sea trout and, after an afternoon of heavy rain, I made my plans to fish. With the stream in spate the inflow of peaty water had stained the bay, creating perfect fishing conditions. Several fish were in evidence on arrival and I felt confident that I would catch fish.

On the first cast a good sized sea trout followed the fly right to the beach. Unfortunately, it showed little inclination to feed. Twenty minutes later, a second fish hit the fly hard, surfaced in a spray of white water, jumped once and threw the fly clear of its jaw. Obviously I was disappointed but I now knew my choice of fly would catch fish and this gave me that edge of confidence that all anglers require.

I was unaware of time passing by this stage but, as the sky began to brighten, I realised that the semi-twilight period was just about over, which meant that I had little time left to catch a fish. Luckily the trout decided to play ball. Two casts and then I hit a big fish that took the fly down close to the sea bed. Typical of all good sized sea trout, this fish shifted into top gear the second it felt the hook, swirling away to the right, obviously intent on gaining sanctuary in a distantly visible raft of seaweed.

Sea trout always seem to have an uncanny knack of knowing exactly where the local snags are located and this fish obviously had every intention of burying itself in the kelp. I had just as much intention of stopping it. By shifting position I was able to change the angle of pull, and with only a few inches to spare I turned the fish from its objective. The trout ran out in a great smooth circle, taking line and backing from the fly reel and for a while we fought a give and take battle but, as always, constant rod pressure began to wear the fish down. Twice I saw the white of its belly, always a sure sign that a fish is well on its way to being exhausted.

Soon it was within reach of my landing net and, as I lifted it clear of the sea, I realised I had taken a great fish from a lonely Orcadian beach in daylight at 2.30 *a.m.* in the morning. Being simply a visitor to the island I had no way of cooking the fish, nor did I then know anyone I could give it to so, taking all this into consideration, I took the hook from its jaw and gently lowered the trout back into the sea.

Releasing that fish gave me more pleasure than catching it. I watched as it slowly recovered, a wild fish on a wild Island beach. And as it sped off, kicking up a spurt of sand from the bottom with its broad tail, I wished it a long and good life hoping that it found a spawning haven where it could help ensure future trout stocks for those lovely Northern Isles.

Living, as I do, in the New Forest I have many opportunities to fish for sea trout. Local rivers in Hampshire and Dorset, although short in length, have for years been noted for the size and quality of the sea trout they produce. However, during the past decade, constant poaching in the tidal waters has seen a decline both in the numbers of sea trout and in the quality of the fishing. Back in the mid 1960s, when the local fishing was still superb, I was lucky enough to have access to a mile of perfect – although heavily overgrown – water. What that little river lacked in width it often made up in the depth of its sluggish pools, and it was from one of these pools that a local farm labourer pitchforked a 16 pound 9 ounce sea trout.

Fly casting on this river was not easy so – to overcome the problems – I constructed a tiny 7 foot glass-fibre rod which had enough power to play out a reasonable fish in 'bushed up' conditions. This rod could throw a no. 7 line and, by using a short leader, I was usually able to fish in comfort as the majority of fish were taken at short range: my usual technique being to cast downstream from a point above the head of the pool.

By strict fly fishing standards, this technique is to be frowned upon, but on a small wild, unkeepered and unloved river the method is perfectly acceptable. Over a period of years I had caught some nice sea trout from that river, and on several occasions had hooked and lost larger fish than normal and also sighted huge sea trout, some weighing well into double figures. These very big fish had a habit of following my fly without showing the slightest indication of taking it.

On a larger river the fish might well have been induced to take, simply because the fly could be worked over a wider area. In a pool only three or four yards long, however, the effective fishing area is simply too short, with most of the fish simply following out of curiosity. I had learned through experience, that 'fresh run' fish were the most likely takers. My fishing was less than three miles from the estuary and after rain the fresh aggressive fish came up-river fast. These fish were always much more inclined to snap at a fly than fish which had been in the river for several weeks.

To take advantage of fresh-run fish I always tried to visit the river directly after a rainy period, and on one such occasion I caught my big fish. The weather had been stormy for several days. The river had not flooded but it had coloured up, and now it was returning to its normal amber-tinged clarity: near perfect sea trout conditions. Oddly enough, I didn't see a single fish move in the first half a dozen pools. Finally, however, I arrived at a place on the river where, in previous seasons, I had seen some good fish.

The pool itself was slightly longer than normal, and totally shadowed by a canopy of marsh alder. Casting space was strictly limited but – with a little practice, and the occasional loss of a fly – I could usually drop a fly well down the pool. As always, I chose a sparsely dressed black fly, flipping it as neatly as possible down the tunnel of overhanging trees.

In my experience, sea trout prefer a lure which travels rapidly through the water and slow moving lures tend to be ignored. Because of this, I stripped the fly back in fast short pulls, causing it to rise and fall in the water. Nothing happened until I began to raise the rod tip to pull the fly clear of the water. Then I saw a broad flash, as an obviously large sea trout swung across the water flow to snatch at the fly.

To this day I cannot recall feeling the actual take, all I remember is a flash of reflected silver followed by the scream of my reel and a huge echoing splash as the fish jumped clear of the water dangerously close to the tail of the pool. Twice more the fish jumped clear, and each time it was closer to the shallows. Sea trout are not stupid and this one, obviously realising its danger, was attempting to leave the pool as quickly as possible.

Under the circumstances I had no choice but follow the fish. My main problem was that I had no accurate indication of the depth of the water. I soon found out, however, for within seconds of entering the river I was over waist deep in cold water! At no time was I able to keep the rod tip high, as overhanging branches were just too hazardous. Fortunately I was able to apply a great deal of rod pressure using the 'side strain' technique. This helped to slow the fish down, but did not stop it from exiting the pool, floundering down through shallows to enter the pool below.

This second pool was less overgrown and I was finally able to apply full rod pressure to the fish. Having seen the trout several times I knew it was big and imagined its weight to be between 9 and 10 pounds. At this stage of the battle the sea trout had stopped jumping and had begun to circle the pool. It was obviously still full of fight, although I knew it must be starting to weaken.

My little fly rod might have looked flimsy, but it had enough strength in the butt to apply a great deal of pressure. Slowly but surely the fish began to lose ground. I managed to turn it several times but, knowing its size, did not want to force the issue and lose my fish as a result. As the minutes ticked away, the fish weakened steadily, finally surfacing, totally spent, with hardly enough strength left to flick its great square tail.

I always carry a big net when fishing for sea trout. For even on rivers where most rod-caught fish are small there is always the chance of a monster. Now, with the big net fully extended, I slid the fish gently over the cord rim and my long battle was over. Later, at home, that fish weighed in at a few ounces under twelve pounds. My best sea trout to date, and proof of the sort of fish that can run tiny local rivers.

On another occasion, I arrived at the pool an hour before sunset, taking up a position where I could see but not be seen. As sea trout pools go, this one was near perfect: a long deep section tapering to the tail-end shallows, with a fast glide under the opposite bank. The river was not large but it had enough depth to hold good fish, and a reputation for producing plenty of good sea trout.

With full dark only minutes away, I turned my head to watch a gliding barn owl and missed the first sign of fish activity for that night. Returning my attention to the river I saw that a fish had moved under the far bank, at a point just to the side of a fast ripple. The temptation was to start casting at once but I had long since learned to bide my time. Patience is a watchword for sea-trout fighting, and it's the man who waits longest who usually catches the most fish. Sure enough, fish began to move steadily: their main activity being centred just above the tail of the pool.

This particular river is always full of minnows and I suspected that it was these rather than a fly hatch that was stimulating the activity. I had already tied on a rather sparse black fly that had a silver-wound body. In the light of day this fly does not look much but, in my experience, sea trout are no respecters of the flytier's art and the more drab a fly looks, the better it appears to catch fish.

My first cast of the night produced a sharp take but the fish obviously came short and did not bite the hook. For a moment or two the fish in the pool stopped moving, but again I waited and within a few minutes fish were once again more in evidence. Two casts later the black fly was taken hard and fast by a fish that reacted in typical sea-trout style by leaping straight out of the water before starting its first run. By the sound it made and the feel of it I knew it was small: taking this into consideration, I decided to bully it to the net for fighting a fish can be fun, but it can also ruin the pool for the remainder of a night.

Fortunately my leader was heavy enough to withstand the strain and, in less than two minutes, I slipped my net under a fresh run fish which – I estimated – weighed a fraction over 1 pound. With the fish in my bag I sat back and waited for the others to resume feeding.

By midnight I had taken two more nice little fish and missed a third on the strike. The tatty black fly obviously had 'fish appeal' and as long as it continued to produce fish I had no intention of changing patterns. As often happens, the sea trout ceased to move and I took the opportunity to broach my flask of coffee and eat my food. Then, at around 2.30 in the morning, I eased back into position which put me within comfortable casting range of the deepest part of the pool.

The pre-dawn hours often produce the larger fish and with this in mind I began casting. For over 30 minutes nothing happened then, just when I felt that I might have made a mistake in fishing the deeper water, my fly was taken firmly by a large confident fish.

Big sea trout seldom rush at a fly; they simply ease up behind it, open their mouths and suck it in. Unlike my earlier fish, this one did not indulge in any aerobatics, instead it made a long, surging run up the pool and, at one stage, I thought it would attempt to leave the pool completely. Luckily, this didn't occur, instead the fish put its head down and began to bang the taut leader with its obviously large tail.

Big sea trout often do this and, as usual, I began to worry about the condition of my nylon leader. I knew that the slightest nick in the nylon would lead to a lost fish and cursed myself for not having renewed the leader during my rest period. Fortunately my leader was obviously still in good condition and the fish abandoned its tail banging, making a long circled run round the pool.

This suited me perfectly, giving me every opportunity to apply maximum rod pressure. In all the trout circled the pool no less than five times before trying its tail-banging routine again. This time it contented itself with just slapping the leader with its tail and I knew it was beginning to weaken.

This prompted me to increase the rod pressure, a ploy that worked. The fish still had the strength to run, but it had lost its speed and much of its power. The fish had not surfaced, up to this time, now it came up in a sluggish roll and I knew I had it beaten. Within minutes I had it in the net and up on the bank. Not a monster but at just under 7 pounds it was a grand fish for that river.

More in hope than expectancy I carried on casting until dawn but did not raise another fish. Obviously my prolonged struggle to land the big one had put all the others down. Still who was I to fuss, I had four fish in the bag, one of them big enough to warrant cold smoking. The night had been more than kind to me.

Hybrids and Others

Quite apart from the rainbow and the, now less common, brown trout some 'put and take' waters are stocked with more exotic fish, such as the American brook trout, the tiger trout, the cheetah and the golden rainbow. All of these, with the exception of the golden rainbow, provide first class sport: the tiger trout being the most aggressive of the bunch.

American Brook Trout

These fish, which are in fact not hybrid but a species of char, are now long established in Britain, but unfortunately, they have not become nearly as widespread as rainbow trout. Brook trout are voracious fish and all those that I have caught have hit the fly hard, usually hooking themselves in the process.

I have been lucky enough to fish for brook trout on a variety of waters, ranging from small day-ticket fisheries to a very hallowed and expensive stretch of the River Test. Brook trout have been taken in Britain up to a little over 5 pounds in weight. However, most rod caught specimens weigh between two and three pounds, and anything over this size can be regarded as a big fish.

In my experience, brook trout tend to be bottom feeders. They will rise occasionally, but are much more likely to fall to a nymph or a lure than a dry fly.

I can always recall my excitement the first time I had the

Three fine brook trout from the River Test.

chance to fish for this species. In those days the Bossington estate at Houghton in Hampshire had a lake which was occasionally let on a day-ticket basis, and the river keeper Tim Baker telephoned me to say that he had a day open for three rods and would I be interested?

Within a couple of hours I had organised two other anglers, and the day was firmly booked. This was my first visit to Bossington Lake, although I knew its reputation which was good. On arrival, we found it a delightful fishery, cut from a vast peat bog and filled from a carrier of the Test.

It had matured into a pretty, narrow lake which had become both an angler's and a naturalist's dream. The bird life there is interesting and varied, and during the day I was able to watch a pair of barn owls quartering the sedge beyond the lake while, behind me, over the high ground no less than four buzzards soared and wheeled in endless circles, their broad wings and wild cry identifying them to even the most novice of bird watchers.

My two companions on this day were Bryn Hammond and Ray Scholes. Bryn, a master mariner, and Ray, a master carpenter, were socially and temperamentally as different as chalk and cheese, but angling breaks down such barriers, and with a rod in our hands and the prospect of a day's fishing ahead the three of us chattered away like schoolchildren.

The lake reputedly held a good head of American brook trout, and our plan was to try to catch a few so that I could photograph them for my library. With this in mind, we split up to cover as much water as possible. Bossington is not a large lake, but it tends to wind about like a section of river and to make things even more interesting it has two islands, which effectively split the top section of the lake into four distinct pieces of narrow, but deep and fishy-looking, water.

None of us then knew much about 'brookies', although Bryn who had fished in the States believed that they showed a particular liking for deep water. I had also read a little about the species, and from this had gleaned that they liked to make use of any cover offered by the banks of any water they lived in. Taking this into consideration, I chose to cast along a section of bank which dropped into dark and obviously deep water. All this occurred long before I developed my Dog Nobbler and my favourite all-round pattern then was a leaded

Netting a brookie.

shrimp, a fly which will catch fish on any water I have ever visited.

Leaded shrimp come in a variety of colours. My favourite being the golden or green variations, rather than the more usual bright orange. Taking into consideration the peaty colour of the water, I chose a leaded golden shrimp which I cast as far along the bank as I could.

Leaded shrimp sink fast, and the second I thought it had reached the bottom I began that twitching short retrieve which most fish find irresistible. On this occasion I had only twitched the shrimp twice when it was taken with a wallop. The savageness of the take – and the speed with which the fish tore off, out into the lake – convinced me that I had hooked a brook trout but, ten minutes later, I was netting a 4½ pound rainbow which had fought harder and longer than any trout of its size I have ever caught before.

During this battle I had been too engrossed to notice that both Bryn and Ray were stuck into good fish. I soon discovered, however, that both of them had caught the coveted brook trout we had come for. Having taken a roll of film of these fish, I returned to my fishing and on the third cast caught my first-ever brook trout. This fish, which weighed just on two pounds, hit my fly so hard that I thought it would be a monster. Despite its savage take the fight style of the brookie was not that impressive. However, I was still delighted to catch the fish, and spent much time admiring its green, gold sides and minute magenta spots.

An angler who has never seen a freshly caught brook trout cannot possibly appreciate just how beautiful its subtle colours can be. Unfortunately these colours fade quickly and the fish once dead soon becomes a drab looking creature. As I recall, we all had a limit bag on that first day, of rainbows, brooks and beautiful brown trout. I vividly remember taking a picture of the whole bag, a photograph which fully illustrated the varied coloration of the trout charm.

Having caught my first brook trout I set about catching them on a regular basis. All anglers have brief obsessions for a particular species and, for a while, my obsession was for brookies. Later that season, Tim Baker – the Bossington keeper – offered me a day on the main river. I knew this lovely stretch of the Test intimately from grayling fishing in the winter, but had never had the opportunity to fish it for trout.

The month was August, and the weather was hot and bright: hardly a trout day, but as I was not in a position to choose I set off, as always, in high hopes. In those days the Bossington fishery was stocked with brown and rainbow trout, and some specially selected American brook trout. I had no idea as to the density of brook trout stocked, but I hoped to find at least one good fish during the day. I found four, weighing a total of 11 ½ pounds!

Having parked my car and deposited surplus tackle and my lunch in the fishing hut, I started off up river in search of rising or positioned trout and found one. I could see the shadow of a good fish beyond a point where a carrier flowed in.

The rules of the fishery were dry fly or nymph, and I chose to fish nymph on a floating line. The positioned fish was obviously on the feed but at sub-surface level, for I could see it swing right or left to intercept food but not once did it make any attempt to take a fly from the surface. I had little idea of what it was feeding on, and whatever it was I still had to guess at the colour. I am quite convinced that trout become preoccupied with the colour of a nymph rather than its size or shape. My guess was that it would be taking black or green and I chose to fish black.

The fly I used is a nasty of my own invention which I call a 'Nothing in Particular'. Simple in construction, it is made up of copper wire wound round a hook, over which is wrapped four strands of peacock herl, tied off at the head and overwrapped with a spiral of copper wire. The finished fly is a humpbacked little beast that looks like nothing in particular, hence its name. Basically it is a cross between a copper nymph and a snail imitator, and what it lacks in appearance it makes up for in fish appeal.

False casting to gain distance, I dropped the fly a yard ahead of the fish and as my nymph started to sink, I saw the fish move up to intercept it. After a short sharp battle I netted a near three pounder, a brook trout in immaculate condition. Until the fish was ready for netting, I had no idea as to its identity but naturally I was delighted with my catch, and off I went in search of more of the same.

I stuck to the same fly pattern throughout the day and, as I

Tiger trout, showing its striped markings.

Tiger Trout

The tiger trout is a highly coloured, much sought after hybrid, produced by crossing American brook and brown trout. The end product is an aggressive, pike-jawed fish which smashes rather than eats a lure and then does its utmost to break the rod or line in its battle to be free. I have caught tiger trout from the Test carrier stream at Broadlands, from a small lake at Alresford and also from the two lakes at Nythe, near Alresford.

said earlier, I finished with two brace of the finest brookies I have ever seen. Having caught these lovely fish I was then able to allow my obsession with brook trout slowly to fade away.

The best tiger trout I have caught so far weighed 4 pounds 4 ounces but I have photographed the two largest specimens yet caught in this country: both came from Nythe Lake and weighed 5 pounds 4 ounces, the other 5 pounds 2 ounces. The

The author's best tiger to date, 4 pounds 4 ounces.

co-owner of the lake, Dave Reilly, is a man who really knows how to produce fine fish, with tiger trout being one of his specialities. A tiger trout in peak condition is a spectacular fish and whenever I fish Nythe I am always on the lookout for a skulking tiger. I say skulking for like its part parent – the brookie – tigers like deep water and cover.

At Nythe, where the water is gin clear, the fish spend much of their time inside the shelter of undercut banks or under weed rafts. Tiger trout are often faddish about lure colours, and most of my fish have been taken on orange or white Dog Nobblers. The Nobbler obviously attracts all types of trout, but tigers seem to show more interest in this than in any other lure.

I said earlier that the tiger is a pike-like fish and this is very true. Tigers like to lurk under cover, from where they can ambush passing fish or insect life, and many of my better tiger trout have been caught from almost directly under my feet. Due to the clarity of the water at Nythe, I have been able to study the tigers' reaction to the lure. While both rainbow and brown trout have a tendency to follow a Nobbler, trying to decide what to do, tigers rarely follow. Having sighted the lure and made their decision, they simply rush the fly, chomping their heavy jaws hard over it. This is exactly what occurred with my 4 pound 4 ounce fish.

The trout had taken up a position just in front of a section of undercut bank. Once in a while it would come out, make a short inspection tour of its territory then swim back to its retreat. The passage of a rainbow or brownie through that territory was guaranteed to bring it out, probably to make certain the interloper left the premises as quickly as possible.

Having seen this behaviour pattern repeated three or four times I waited for a fish to pass through the area, dropping my orange Nobbler into its wake. Sure enough, as the stranger passed the tiger's hideout, the tiger shot into view just as my orange Nobbler rippled past. The fish did not hesitate; it struck the fly ferociously and, as I raised the rod point and set the hook, the startled tiger picked up speed and took off across the lake as though its tail was on fire.

Most brown trout can be bullied and a fair percentage of rainbows as well, but you most certainly cannot force the issue with an angry tiger.

A brace of triploids: the trout of the future?

This one reacted in typical tiger style. Long runs, splashy jumps and masses of heavy head shaking which made me fear for my leader. Finally, however, it was all over and that fish was in the net. Looking back, I feel I should have had the fish set up as it would have looked splendid in a nice bow-fronted case. In actual fact I had it cold smoked which, on reflection, was not such a bad idea either.

Cheetah Trout

Yet another hybrid, this particular fish is a speciality of just one British fishery, Avington, near Winchester in Hampshire. Produced by crossing rainbow and brown trout, the resulting hybrid is a spectacular fish, which has been taken to over 9 pounds on conventional fly tackle.

I have never caught one of these fish, although I understand from people who have that they feed and fight like a normal rainbow trout.

Golden Rainbow

This is a throw-off from a standard strain of rainbows. Dave Walford of Whitchurch, produced the first specimens and has managed to establish a breeding strain of these yellow-gold fish.

I have caught them from two fisheries, Leominstead and Rooksbury Mill, both in Hampshire. In shape, size and temperament, the golden rainbows are similar to standard rainbow trout. Unfortunately, the ones I have caught have all been poor fighters.

Grayling

No book concerned with fly fishing would be complete without mention of the grayling, popular with anglers, *thymallus thymallus,* and a 'game' species found in Britain, Scandinavia and Middle Europe. Unpopular with riparian owners, the grayling inhabits the same world and type of water as the trout. Basically a stream and river fish, the grayling is said to compete with trout for food and, as grayling breed readily if left unchecked, they can soon overrun a good trout water. Unfortunately, in many cases, grayling have been culled so ruthlessly that they no longer exist in waters where they were once common.

Seldom regarded as a lake species grayling have nevertheless been introduced to several lake fisheries, although as yet there has been no evidence of grayling breeding in these lakes. Grayling have much to offer as a sporting species. They rise freely, fight well and make excellent table fish, and I believe that most fly fishermen have a secret liking for grayling and would hate to see them disappear from all our rivers.

At times, when trout become reluctant to rise to the fly, grayling can be counted on to rise freely and, in fact, a good many anglers mistake rising grayling for rising trout. To the experienced angler grayling rises in a very different way to trout. Trout tend to sip a fly gently from the surface while grayling, with their underslung mouth, take a fly with a characteristic slashing motion. To make rise identification even more positive, the rising grayling invariably leaves a single large air bubble on the surface. Grayling can also be counted on to rise in extremes of weather, and on the River

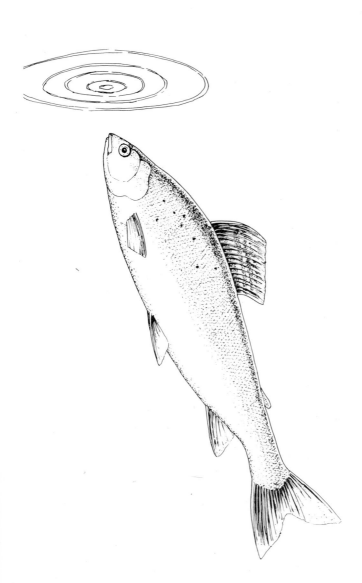

FIGURE 18   A female grayling.

Test I have seen large grayling rise both in the middle of a winter snow storm and at midday during a baking August.

The nicest way to catch grayling is to fish with dry fly only. Grayling are not fussy feeders and almost any small dry fly will take fish. Iron Blue Dun, Coch-y-Bonddu, and a Black Gnat will all catch fish, even when they do not conform to the fly hatch in progress. Once feeding, grayling are difficult fish to put down so they make perfect practice for the novice fly caster. Unlike trout, which are easily alarmed, rising grayling will put up with poor casting, splashy presentation, even a fly that drags across the surface.

Grayling are normally shoal fish although, in the case of extra large fish, the 'shoal' may consist of only a couple of fish of similar size. If you hook and then lose one fish, the chances are that the remainder will cease feeding.

Grayling can sometimes be seen feeding on or close to the bottom. Under these circumstances upstream nymph is the perfect way to take fish. Almost any nymph can be used, the best being the Killer Bug, Damsel, Shellback Shrimp or Pheasant Tail Nymph.

A grayling showing its sail-like dorsal fin.

On days when clear water and perfect light conditions prevail, it is fun to cast and catch preselected fish. Under these circumstances grayling can be induced to take by using the nymph just before it reaches the fish. This 'induced take' routine really stimulates the grayling to hit the nymph hard. Grayling can often be found in all sections of a river and I have taken 2 pound plus fish from glides of less than twelve inches deep.

The perfect place to find large grayling is in a sudden dip in the river bed (see Figure 19). This sort of 'hole' is seldom easy to fish but it can normally be relied upon to hold better than average specimens. Smaller grayling show a liking for shaded water, while for big bags of medium fish tree-hung pools fish best.

Grayling are worthy of any angler's attention. For a large one hooked in fast water can fight as well as a trout of double its weight, and they make excellent eating. One of the best ways of cooking your catch is to wash and gut the fish then dry thoroughly. Rub over with coarse salt and then grill. When cooked the skin and scales can be lifted off easily, leaving the white fish perfectly exposed.

Every grayling angler has a favourite river. In Britain, some

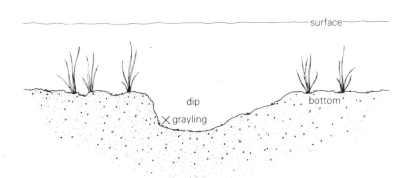

FIGURE 19 Although grayling can be found throughout a river, large grayling prefer dips in the river bed. These can be difficult to fish but are worth the effort.

love the rocky waters of the north; others the chalk streams of Hampshire. Having fished for grayling in many places, one river draws me more than all of the others I have known: this is the River Dever, a tributary of the River Test.

Famous in its own right as a trout water, the Dever is very different to the average chalk stream being, for the most part, fairly shallow and yet sluggish in comparison to the nearby Test. Full of food, the Dever supports a good head of large brown trout, plus a superb head of giant grayling. I have seen shoals of over a hundred Dever grayling, all large fish and all feeding in a comparatively small section of river.

As I said earlier, the beauty of grayling is that they are a free rising species, which often feed well at times when trout studiously ignore the fly. And over the years I have had great fun catching dozens of grayling over 2 pounds in weight, with a fair number of fish within a fraction of the three pound mark.

Most of these extra-large grayling have come from hatch pools, where the water has been slightly deeper and well oxygenated. The problem with this sort of pool is that the rush of water through the hatch mouth makes it extremely difficult to present a dry fly correctly to the waiting fish.

I remember one such hatch pool, where water tumbled through a narrow throat then opened out into a broad pool. Years of water action had scoured out the bottom of the pool, to a depth greater than the actual stonework of the hatch. This meant that below the water flow the fish could lie in a deep pocket of slack water: a perfect position for the fish, but a practically impossible one for the angler.

A careful inspection of the lie showed that it held a couple of reasonable trout and one huge grayling. The trout did not interest me but the grayling did. Time and again, during the course of the season, I had tried to entice that fish to come up, but on each occasion the fast-moving surface water caught my leader and skittered my fly unnaturally across the surface.

A small grayling might have come up for such a fly. The big chap, on the other hand, showed no such inclination to commit suicide. I often spoke to the river keeper about this fish, and about my lack of success, and like me he began to show an interest in the grayling. Finally, with only a few days to go before the end of the season, I fished my way up to the

Author with two good grayling from the River Test.

hatch pool and found, to my amazement, the large grayling out of its water lie and feeding avidly in a small slack at the edge of the mainstream. From the way that fish fed I could see that it was taking full advantage of a hatch of darkish insects.

Quickly changing to an artificial of approximately similar size and colour, I made my cast to drop the fly slightly ahead of the feeding fish. The grayling did not even wait for my fly to work back over its position. Instead it eased forward, rose with confidence and sucked in the fly, leaving the usual 'grayling bubble' in the centre of the rise ring.

Hooking the fish was easy but, like all large grayling, the fish was off like a flash, diving as fast as it could for its sanctuary below the stonework of the hatch. Once into deep water, it used its huge sail-like dorsal fin as a drogue, defying me to prise it back up through the main current. When first hooked, a fighting grayling can be a difficult fish to control. This one was no exception, it just didn't show any inclination to budge.

Finally, however, it began to give ground then bolted out of

121

the hole, shot right round the pool and headed off downstream at full speed. From this stage on, rod pressure coupled with line drag quickly wore down the grayling until it was ready for netting.

Most Dever grayling are bright silver, this one was much darker and its dorsal fin was enormous. It was the best grayling I'd ever taken. The rule of the river was that all grayling were to be killed but I knew, before I'd even netted this one, that I would return it, even if it meant never fishing the river again. After all that fish had haunted my trips until, finally, it made a mistake, and who was I to take its life. What I did take, however, was a scale from its shoulder, before easing the fly from its lips and slipping it gently back into the river. Later the scale showed the fish to be 14 years old, and its weight? Who knows? Over three pounds certainly, but I didn't care.

A Word About Salmon

Even though this is a book about trout fishing I want to write a short piece about salmon, for these fish provide a logical progression in a fishing career that many trout fishermen make.

Salmon fishing is generally regarded as a rich man's sport. This may well be true when speaking of major rivers like the Spey, the Dee, the Test and the magical rivers of Iceland and Norway, but there are other waters, small wild rivers in

A Broadlands salmon for the author, taken on fly.

Wales, Cornwall, Scotland and Ireland where good salmon fishing is often obtainable at modest cost.

Much of this water belongs to country hotels or to local associations and in many cases day tickets are available.

There are also one or two stillwaters now being opened that operate on a 'put and take' basis, where salmon are stocked in the same way as trout. Such landlocked salmon fisheries are very successful in America, but I have my reservations about the success of such fisheries in Britain, especially as Britain has this reserve of wild (and relatively cheap) salmon rivers.

Hopefully time will prove me to be a pessimist but, as yet, I can find no evidence that stillwater salmon fisheries are going to be viable, either from a fishery owner's or an angler's point of view.

Rods

Salmon fly rods are designed for use with one or two hands, according to the style of casting employed. The double-handed variety are usually 12-14 foot long, and certainly over 11 foot.

The ideal length for an all round rod, in my view, is 12½-13 foot and this – coupled with a double tapered, size 9 line – is suitable for fishing most of the salmon waters in Britain, Europe or America.

The principal materials used for salmon fly rods are: built cane, tubular glass fibre, carbon fibre and boron. Many salmon fishermen have a preference for a rod of built cane, particularly a model with spliced joints which (so called, because the sections are spliced together with binding tape) form a very strong joint.

This spliced joint is of great value in Spey casting, a form of roll cast used when obstructions behind the angler prevent a normal back cast. The Spey style exerts a twisting force along the rod, but spliced joints resist the urge of the rod's sections to twist at the joints and so lose alignment.

Carbon fibre fly rods, although expensive, are becoming increasingly popular. They cast as well as a top quality built cane model, while being much lighter to handle. Their small diameter is a great advantage in windy conditions, where a thicker built cane rod would offer wind resistance.

Tubular glass is still popular. It gives a serviceable rod, is much cheaper than either carbon fibre or built cane and although heavier than carbon fibre, has the advantage of lightness over a built cane rod.

Most salmon fly rods today have a 'through action' that can be felt from the tip to the butt. A tip with this fairly rigid action is required because of the need to 'mend' line, that is straighten it out, when the strength of the current varies at different points across the stream, and the line is pulled into a bow shape. This pulling, in turn, carries the fly back across the flow at an unnatural angle.

If this happens then the fishermen must roll the line to 'mend' it, and a heavy tipped rod enables a weighty length of double tapered line to be lifted off the water and 'mended' with reasonable ease.

Single handed fly rods of ten foot or longer are suited to smaller rivers, where smaller flies are used.

Reels

The size of reel used for salmon fishing depends on the rod, river and line weight to be used. Remember that the reel must be large enough to hold at least a hundred yards of backing line of 15 to 20 or 25 pounds breaking strain.

Gaffs and Tailers

Salmon can be landed with a net but most anglers prefer to use a gaff or a tailer. Both are light, sure and convenient, but each possesses disadvantages that need careful consideration before purchase.

Collapsible or telescopic gaffs are the most popular. These range from those of lightweight alloy to heavy brass or steel models: those made from alloy cost less, but tend to corrode rapidly. Good quality gaffs have steel or heavy gauge brass sections, with a firm rubber or cork handle and the added safety precaution of a leather thong that can be looped over the wrist. If this is not fitted to the gaff when purchased it can easily be added.

Gaff heads are made from steel. The point of a gaff needs

protection and a brass safety cup, into which the point will fit, is the safest device; never use a loose piece of cork pushed onto the point, this isn't enough and serious accidents have occurred.

The gape (or distance) between the point of the gaff and its shank is important: too little and it will be impossible to draw the point home, too much and it will affect the balance and cause the handle to turn in use. Cheap gaffs – consisting of a wooden pole to which a head is firmly screwed, and then close whipped with copper wire – make a good alternative.

To gaff salmon, an angler needs a steady hand and a lot of common sense. Undue movement made by the gaff as it approaches the fish will often cause the salmon to lunge away. Only when the fish is lying quietly on the surface should the gaff point be set, preferably in the jaw rather than along the stomach or shoulder of the beaten fish. Once the point is driven home, the fish should be lifted straight onto the bank in a single movement.

The gaff is effective, but so too is the tailer. This uses a grip around the 'wrist' of the tail to hold and lift a fish onto the bank. A tailer consists of a heavy length of stiff, cabled steel bent and held open by a thin, flexible wire that connects to the handle. When the fish is played out, the open wire loop is slid over the tail, and back onto the 'wrist' immediately before the caudal fin. Once in place, the handle of the tailer is raised sharply and the wire noose immediately clamps tightly into the flesh. The fish can then be lifted clear of the water by the same vertical lift that is used with a gaff.

Salmon Flies

As salmon do not feed while travelling up to their spawning grounds, salmon flies are designed to imitate fish rather than to represent a natural insect.

This need has led to a wide range of flashy fly designs, all of which will catch on their day. Colour has always been regarded as important, of course, but as almost all anglers have their own specific theories as to what makes a good salmon fly almost every known colour combination has been tried.

In spite of all this variety of colour, there is a great similarity among the flies as to shape and style, for the modern salmon angler seems to prefer tube fly patterns, particularly those which incorporate a gaudy colour combination.

Such flies as Jock Scott, Black Doctor, Blue Charm, Thunder and Lightning, Durham Ranger, Green Highlander, Green King, Logie and many others have become well-known fish producers, carried by most salmon anglers as part of their normal fly selection.

Modern flies with hair wings still retain the original brightness of the traditional patterns, and the hairs used for the wings are usually dyed the same bright shades of red, blue, yellow, green and orange. There are exceptions, where the fibres are left in their natural colour and the Blue Charm is a good example of this, with the teal and mallard flank feathers of the original pattern being replaced by either brown bucktail fibres or brown squirrel tail fibres according to size of hook. The hair winged version of the Blue Charm is the Hairy Mary.

The size of a salmon fly is more important than its colour: the size used depending largely on the height, temperature and colour of the water, and on prevailing weather conditions. If fish are seen to follow a fly then shy away, the chances are that the lure is too big.

I always prefer to start fishing with a small fly and increase the size if necessary. As a general rule, the bigger the river the larger the fly. A large fly is useful in coloured water, in very rough water, or in deep runs that have a dark coloured bottom. Where wind, light and temperature are constant, a medium sized fly is best while low clear water calls for a much smaller dull coloured fly pattern.

In addition to the general patterns, there are others designed for specific rivers. The best known of these are the 'Spey' patterns, tied with rather drab materials. Such flies are used in the early part of the season, when temperatures can be at almost freezing point. Spey flies are dressed lightly on very large hooks, 3 inches being quite common. The combination of light dressing and heavy hook means that the flies sink deep and fast bringing them quickly down to the level of salmon lying close to the bottom.

One of the most important features of these flies is the

extreme mobility of their hackles and wings, which gives them a very lifelike appearance when they are worked in the water.

Prawn or Shrimp is also a good pattern, designed to imitate the natural food of the salmon during its life in salt water. These flies can be very successful during the early part of the season, the theory being that they are snatched at by the salmon through force of habit rather than from a true desire to feed.

Irish salmon flies are usually more heavily dressed than standard patterns, being tied with warm rich colours ideally suited to the peaty waters of that country's rivers.

Tube Flies

Although the tube fly has been available for many years, its popularity is a recent occurrence. The tube fly, as its name implies, consists of a length of tubing (polythene or metal) round which are whipped hair or simulated hair fibres from the tails of different animals.

Orthodox salmon fly bodies are generally added to the tubes, and long fibred hackles may be used as an addition to the hair fibres. One of the first tube flies was the Parker Tube Fly, since when all flies have followed a very similar style and method of construction.

Other patterns quickly followed, a typical example being the Stoat Tail, which consisted merely of fibres from the tail of a stoat, whipped round one end of a piece of tubing. Variations soon began to appear, and these usually either took the form of additions to the tube body itself, using silk and tinsel as coverings, or the addition of coloured hairs different to those used on the original Stoat Tail.

Marabou and ostrich herl body feathers are good examples of the feathers now used for lying tube flies, as all have long flowing fibres which work well in the water when the fly is fished. To add weight, some tubes are made of brass, into which a polythene tube has been inserted and these are ideal for use in deep or fast water.

Tube flies are used in conjunction with a treble hook, which is tied to the end of the leader. The tube is then slid down the leader, tail end first until it is stopped by the eye of the treble hook: the tube being allowed to run free on the leader, a factor which has a double advantage. *One,* when the fly is being fished the pressure of water holds it tight to the treble hook, whereas when the hook is taken by a fish the reverse applies and, *two,* the drag caused by the fish's run drive the tube up the leader towards the line. This prevents the fish from using the fly body to lever out the hook and also stops the fly from being destroyed during the battle.

Conventional fly tying equipment can be used to make tube flies, if used with one or two sizes of tapered, eyeless salmon hooks, on which the tubes can be slid to facilitate tying. Hook sizes 4, 2 and 2/0 should cope with most tube diameters.

To prevent the treble from hanging at an angle to the tube during casting, a small piece of polythene tubing can be fixed over the hook end of each tube when it is completed, the eye of the treble can then be drawn into this before the angler starts to fish. Unless you take this precaution, the hook can snag itself on the leader in front of the tube, resulting in a number of useless casts.

The easiest tube fly to tie is a hair winged pattern, known as a Hairy Mary. To tie this fly, first press the tube onto a tapered hook shank, taking great care not to split or damage the end of the tube.

The bend of the hook is then held in the vice and tying silk wound round the tube. The tying silk should then be wound back the other way, and followed with the body silk and tinsel rib in that order. A layer of the tying silk is then put on the remaining piece of tubing to form a bed for the ends of the hair fibres which are to be added.

The wing of this fly is made from brown bucktail or squirrel tail. The hairs are cut off by twisting a small bunch of them together and trimming them close to the root. Any soft fur – found at the base of most hair fibres – should be prised out with a dubbing needle. The size of the head should be kept to a minimum, to prevent a bow wave when the fly is worked through the water. The bunch of fibres is now tied in on top of the tube and the waste ends cut off after each bunch of fibres is tied in as this makes for a neat finish.

The tube is then rolled round the hook shank, bringing to the top the next portion which is to be covered by hairs. Another bunch of fibres is then tied in, the turns of silk being to the immediate right of the turns securing the first bunch.

Continue in this way until the whole tube has been covered.

Placing the silk turns to the right as each bunch is tied in will help keep down the size of the head, for a fly with a bulky head looks unbalanced and seldom works well. Finally, a single layer of silk should be wound round all fibres where they are tied in, this forms a neat head and gives a uniform angle to the fibres. All the waste ends of the fibres were cut off as the body progressed, so now just whip finish the fly and apply one or two coats of thin clear varnish to the head.

All the silk whippings should be well soaked in the varnish to stop them unravelling in use.

If the tube fly requires a hackle in front, this is wound at the point where the first bunch of fibres was tied in, using the fingers of your left hand to make sure that all the hackle fibres are drawn to the rear. Wind a few turns of silk over their base, so that these contain the hair as closely as possible.

Body hackles can be added as with a normal fly. I find, however, that the sparser the dressing the more it appears to attract fish. Final fly detail is, of course, up to the individual angler. The truth is that if you have confidence in a pattern you will usually catch fish with it.

My Methods

I have had some good days spinning on the Test at Broadlands, on the Hampshire Avon, the Dorset Stour and the Frome. My most memorable salmon fishing has, however, been with the fly on various 'little' rivers. I remember best one such day on the top end of the Fowey river in Cornwall.

The Fowey is a typical West Country river, rugged, bushed up and by no means easy to fish but, on occasion, its delightful pools produce excellent salmon fishing, particularly after long periods of rain.

I was fortunate enough to have an invitation to fish a short stretch of some private water which included one or two delectable pools. The water condition was near perfect, and the strongly coloured water of the previous few days had gone, leaving just a taint of peaty water in its wake: like a fine whisky which, to my eye, promised the chance of a fish.

The Fowey seldom produces large fish, 5 to 7 pounds being

about normal. However, a lively fish of this size in such confined surroundings can provide thrilling sport, as I had learned on past occasions.

I began operations at what I call the throat pool. In reality a decent sized, heavily overhung pool with a very narrow entrance. The tail end of this pool being wide and shallow.

My rod on this occasion was a ten foot carbon reservoir rod, capable of throwing a no. 8 line. Basically my rod was too long for the section of river I was fishing but, not being in a position to afford a different rod for every water, I had chosen this rod to cover most of my needs.

The fly was of my own tying, a sparsely dressed tail pattern, which resembled little in nature but appeared to have salmon appeal. Having moved into the only casting position available to me, I waited twenty minutes to let any disturbance my arrival had made quieten down. Then, with little more than a rod and a half's length of line in the air, I made my first cast to drop the drab hairwing fly into what I hoped was the holding area of the pool.

Nothing moved. A dozen barren casts later and I was convinced that the pool was empty: the odd native brown trout maybe, but certainly no salmon. Despite my misgivings, I decided on just one more cast and, as the fly swung round and down stream, I saw my leader slide purposefully across the flow. Raising my rod point, I set the hook solidly into a fish which shot upstream, turned at the narrow entrance and tore off down, crossing the shallows at high speed with me in hot pursuit.

The water below the pool opened into a long glide of 50 yards or so in length and approximately two and a half feet in depth. Overhanging trees made it impossible for me to keep the rod high, and I was forced to drop the rod sideways to apply full strain to the angry fish. Fortunately I was using a strong leader, and I knew that if I could contain the fish in the long glide I could ultimately subdue and tail it.

Time means little when playing a good fish and this is particularly true when one is fishing alone. All I knew was that as the minutes passed the rod strain and line drag were taking their toll on the salmon's strength.

Twice I felt my leader scrape across some submerged object, for a hooked salmon is more than capable of deliberately chafing through a leader on any handy obstruction it can find. Fortunately my leader held and, finally, I had the fish under total control. Minutes later it was wallowing within reach so I unhitched my tailer, positioned the fish and within seconds it was mine. Its weight just six pounds, its condition near perfect. Less than a week in the river and aided on its run by high water, this salmon had made it upriver with hardly a scale out of place.

Some years ago I had an eight pounder from a river in the West of Ireland in very different circumstances. The river was one of those wild, rocky short-lived rivers which abound in Ireland, and when I caught my salmon it was in a rocky outlet pool with seaweed covered rocks, where shoals of pollack and, at night, sea trout were my main quarry.

To be honest, I did not have the slightest idea that salmon could be found in this river: my target being sea trout. I arrived late in the evening, after a splendid farm house supper, to find sea trout leaping in fair numbers and chose a dark fly with a silver-ribbed body. A fly which had stood me in good stead in the past. Starting to false cast I noticed the flash of a heavy fish as it turned on its side behind a sunken boulder. It looked too big for a sea trout and I assumed that in all probability it was a bass.

Not being averse to catching bass on fly tackle, I cast towards the area where the fish had turned, waited for the fly to sink and began to retrieve quite rapidly. My line came taut without moving, and I began to curse my luck at having fouled my fly on rock or weed. Lifting the rod high, to try to dislodge the trapped fly, I was amazed to find the obstruction no more. I was into a fish and a good one, but of what species?

At first the fish was content to cruise round the pool until fearful of the rocks in its path, I tried to apply extra pressure to bring it under control. It was then that I discovered I was fast to a salmon. A salmon which promptly leapt clear of the water and headed out to sea at high speed.

Within seconds all my fly line was out, and much of my backing line with it. Thinking to regain some line, I moved out across the bankside rocks, totally forgetting that the mixture of salt water and freshwater grows a weed so slippery that you can skate on it. More of a slimy moss really than a weed, but enough to skate me neatly into waist deep water.

Luckily there was no one about to laugh at my predicament, and if there had been it would not have mattered, for my only interest was in landing that salmon. Once over the shock of my sudden immersion in cold water, I rather enjoyed the playing of that fish. Slowly but surely it began to give ground and, as it did, I inched my way to a partially submerged ledge. Finally it was over and directly in front of me lay the most pristine salmon I shall ever see. That fish was beyond being fresh, it had not even entered the river proper.

Laying the rod right back over my shoulder, I inched the fish within range, slid it over the rim of my landing net and within seconds was out of the water, up and over the rock ledges to a point well back from the river. I still cannot remember making my exit from the water, I can only recall how anxious I was to get my fish to safety.

My third salmon story concerns a wild, rocky and savage little river on one of the West Coast islands that abound off Scotland. I chose to fly fish and, as usual, I was fishing a drab little tube fly which has a slight tinge of orange/brown about it.

The river, as might be expected, was short with just half a dozen likely pools. The most promising of which was situated in a sort of rocky canyon. This natural cleft was deep and dark, and looked just the place to find a fish. I had no idea of the depth of water, but from the geographical layout of the pool I assumed it held between six and eight foot of peat-stained water.

It was possible at one point to inch down to a position just above water level and it was from here I proposed to fish. The take came instantly, the tube hit the surface and the line began to slide out immediately as a fish snatched at the lure. So confident was the take that I struck automatically, feeling the rod buck as the fish hurtled away downstream.

Looking back I am certain that the darkness of the pool lulled that salmon into a sense of false security. Not once did it attempt to vacate the pool and its dark shelter, instead it swam up and down until, finally, it was worn out by rod spring and line drag. As fights went this one was not spectacular, its drama lay in the awesome nature of the pool itself. The fish weighed 8¼ pounds. Again, not a big fish, but one I shall always remember.

I have caught much larger salmon than the ones described,

but my bigger fish have come on bait, spoon and plug. These fly-caught fish, small as they may be, are the ones I best remember.

Trout Flies – The Essential Dressings

Dry Flies

BLACK GNAT
Hook	12 – 16 standard
Silk	black
Body	stripped peacock herl
Hackle	black cock

DADDY LONGLEGS
Hook	10 – 12 longshank
Silk	brown
Body	green heron herl with strand of pheasant tail (or plastic body of mayfly, tied in)
Legs	knotted pheasant tail, cock feathers
Wings	light ginger cock hackle points
Hackle	red cock

G & H SEDGE
Hook	8 – 12 longshank
Silk	green or black
Body	deer hair, spun on as for Muddler head and trimmed to shape
Under body	dark green seal or orange seal (or leave out if desired)
Hackle	two rusty dun cock hackles, stripped (as antennae)

HAWTHORN
Hook	10 – 12 standard
Silk	black

Body	peacock herl (three strands), or black floss silk, wound over wet varnish
Legs	two strands peacock herl or stiffened thread, tied trailing
Head	single strand black herl
Hackle	two black cock hackles

POND OLIVE

Hook	10 – 14 standard
Silk	grey
Tail	dark blue dun cock fibre from saddle feather
Body	three strands light brown condor herl
Ribbing	silver tinsel
Wing	bunch pale waterhen feather fibre
Hackle	pale brassy blue dun cock

TUPS INDISPENSIBLE

Hook	12 – 16 standard
Tail	pale ginger cock hackle fibre
Body	two parts sheep's wool; seal fur, 2 parts cream, 1 part beige, 1 part red, all mixed
Hackle	pale ginger cock

WALKER'S SEDGE

Hook	8 – 10 longshank
Silk	brown
Body	chestnut coloured ostrich herl (three strands)
Wing	red cock hackles, clipped square
Hackle	two stiff red cock hackles

Wet Flies

BLACK AND PEACOCK SPIDER

Hook	8 – 12 standard
Silk	black
Body	four strands peacock herl
Under body	black floss silk (or fine wire, if required leaded)
Head	black varnish
Hackle	black hen

BLACK ZULU

Hook	10 – 14 standard
Silk	black
Tail	red wool
Body	black wool or seal fur
Ribbing	fine flat silver tinsel
Hackle	black cock, palmered

DUNKELD

Hook	10 – 14 standard
Silk	black or brown
Tail	golden pheasant crest
Body	gold tinsel
Ribbing	gold wire
Wings	mallard
Eye	jungle cock substitute
Hackle	orange hen, palmered

COCH-Y-BONDDU

Hook	12 – 14 standard
Silk	brown
Body	two strands bronze peacock herl
Ribbing	fine gold tinsel
Hackle	coch-y-bonddu cock

GREENWELL'S GLORY

Hook	12 – 14 standard
Silk	yellow
Body	yellow silk rubbed down with cobbler's wax
Ribbing	gold wire
Wings	blackbird, tied sloping
Hackle	coch-y-bonddu cock

MALLARD AND CLARET

Hook	10 – 14 standard (larger for sea trout)
Silk	black
Tail	four golden pheasant tippets
Body	claret seal fur
Ribbing	fine gold wire
Wings	dark bronze mallard
Hackle	claret, red cock or black

SILVER MARCH BROWN

Hook	10 – 14 standard
Silk	brown
Tail	three partridge hackle fibres, speckled
Body	flat silver tinsel
Ribbing	fine silver tinsel
Wings	hen pheasant secondary feather, mottled
Hackle	brown partridge, mottled

TEAL BLUE AND SILVER

Hook	8 – 14 standard
Silk	black, waxed
Tail	four golden pheasant tippets
Body	flat silver tinsel
Ribbing	fine oval silver tinsel
Wings	teal breast feathers
Hackle	bright blue cock hackle

WICKHAM'S FANCY

Hook	12 – 14 standard
Silk	yellow
Tail	fine red game cock fibres
Body	flat gold tinsel
Ribbing	fine gold wire
Wings	dark starling
Hackle	red game cock, palmered

Nymphs

CORIXA

Hook	10 – 12 standard
Silk	brown or black
Body	cream floss, silk or acetate
Ribbing	fine silver wire
Wing cases	brown turkey tail fibres
Head	black varnish
Hackle	grouse hackle

DAMSELFLY NYMPH

Hook	8 – 12 longshank

Silk	green
Tail	three olive cock hackles, tips only
Body	olive seal fur
Thorax	dark olive-brown seal fur
Ribbing	flat gold tinsel
Wing cases	fibre from mallard shoulder feather
Hackle	fibres from grouse hackle, on underneath sloping back

NOTHING IN PARTICULAR

Hook	10 – 12 standard
Silk	black
Body	copper wire wound round shank, covered with few strands of peacock herl
Ribbing	fine copper wire

PHEASANT TAIL NYMPH

Hook	10 – 16 standard
Silk	black
Tail	(see body)
Body	cock pheasant centre-tail fibres, points protruding to provide tail
Ribbing	fine copper wire
Wing cases	dark cock pheasant centre-tail fibres, wound to create thorax then taken over as wing cases
Head	black varnish
Hackle	sparse ginger hen

Lures

ACE OF SPADES

Hook	8 – 12 longshank
Silk	black
Body	black chenille
Ribbing	oval silver tinsel
Wing	black hen, tied as crest matuka style: bronze mallard as overwing
Hackle	guinea fowl

APPETIZER

Hook	8 – 12 longshank
Silk	black
Tail	mixed orange, green and silver mallard fibres
Body	white chenille
Ribbing	silver tinsel
Wing	white marabou herl: grey squirrel as overwing
Hackle	mixed orange, green and silver mallard fibres, on underneath sloping back

BLACK DOG NOBBLER

Hook	8 longshank, offset downwards at eye
Silk	black
Tail	black marabou
Body	black chenille
Ribbing	silver tinsel
Head	shot, or lead wire wound from offset to eye

JERSEY HERD

Hook	8 – 10 longshank
Silk	orange
Tail	peacock herl, from body
Body	glitter wool, peacock herl to form back and tail
Head	strands, twisted of peacock herl
Hackle	orange hen

MUDDLER MINNOW

Hook	8 – 12 longshank
Silk	black
Tail	section of turkey wing
Body	flat gold tinsel
Wings	bunch of grey squirrel tail to form inner wing: sections mottled turkey wing feather to form outer wing
Head	natural deer hair, spun on and clipped (similar to G & H Sedge)

WHISKY FLY

Hook	8 – 10 longshank
Silk	orange
Body	flat gold tinsel
Ribbing	scarlet floss
Wing	orange calftail or orange hackle
Head	scarlet floss
Tag	as above
Hackle	hot orange cock hackle

Flies for Sea Trout

BUTCHER

Hook	6 – 10 standard
Silk	black
Tail	red ibis
Body	silver tinsel
Wings	crow or magpie, tied sloping
Hackle	black hen

Black Zulu (see page 137)

PETER ROSS

Hook	6 – 10 standard
Silk	black, waxed
Tail	five golden pheasant tippets
Body	tail half silver tinsel, forward half red seal fur
Ribbing	fine silver tinsel
Wing	teal breast feathers
Hackle	black hen

Teal Blue and Silver (see page 138)

Index

Numbers in *italic* refer to illustrations, numbers in **bold** to fly dressings.